Praise for *Taming the Dragons*

"A wisdom-filled book which incorporates and underscores the resources available in the Christian faith for personal healing and growth."
—Lars I. Granberg, former president, Northwestern College

"Wilbee offers stories instead of advice, setting each reader free to choose her own heroines and role models . . . Images of womanly strength remain to hearten and challenge the thoughtful."
—Maxine Hancock, author of *Child Sexual Abuse: A Hope for Healing*

"*Taming the Dragons* is a clear, practical, and compelling guidebook on how women can deal creatively with the dragons they face in a patriarchal society. This book provides alternatives to despair and giving up in the face of these difficulties and offers hope instead."
—Morton Kelsey, author of *Psychology, Medicine & Christian Healing* and *Reaching*

"A highly creative approach . . . Wilbee combines biblical characters as well as such familiar stories as *The Wizard of Oz* to bring the reader to understand the *choices* that she has in dealing with the dragons we all face. A great gift book for women facing difficult circumstances."
—Alvera Mickelsen, author of *Women, Authority, and the Bible*

"A captivating book, written in a crisp and caring style, loaded with important 'stuff' for finding a way toward wholeness and the abundant life. Wilbee's warm but confronting insights encourage and empower women (and men) to be their own persons. A marvelous exposition of Jesus' words to us: 'Be wise as serpents and innocent as doves.' "
—William A. Miller, author of *Your Golden Shadow: Discovering and Fulfilling Your Undeveloped Self*

TAMING THE
DRAGONS

$\mathcal{T}$AMING THE $\mathcal{D}$RAGONS

Christian Women
Resolving Conflict

Brenda Wilbee

HarperSanFrancisco
A Division of HarperCollins*Publishers*

TAMING THE DRAGONS: *Christian Women Resolving Conflict*,
© 1992 by Brenda Wilbee. All rights reserved. Printed in the
United States of America. No part of this book may be used
or reproduced in any manner whatsoever without written
permission except in the case of brief quotations embodied
in critical articles and reviews. For information address Harper-
Collins Publishers, 10 East 53rd Street, New York, NY 10022.

FIRST EDITION

Library of Congress Cataloging-in-Publication Data

Wilbee, Brenda.
    Taming the dragons : Christian women resolving conflict /
Brenda Wilbee. — 1st ed.
        p.
    ISBN 0-06-069419-X (alk. paper)
    1. Women, Christian—Religious life.   2. Women—Conduct
of life.   3. Assertiveness in women.   I. Title.
BV4527.W54   1991
248.8′43—dc20   90-55762
                                                                   CIP

92 93 94 95 96 HAD 10 9 8 7   6 5 4 3 2 1

This edition is printed on acid-free paper that meets the American National Standards Institute Z39.48 Standard.

For my sister,

TRESA WILBEE

WIGGINS,

for teaching me I can choose.

$\mathcal{C}$ONTENTS

$\mathcal{A}$CKNOWLEDGMENTS

"I can no other answer make but thanks,
*And thanks, and ever thanks."**

I thank first of all my sister, TRESA WILBEE WIGGINS, for being the first in my life to teach me I have choice. There is no greater gift.

I thank her husband BRUCE W. WIGGINS for taking me to see *The Wizard of Oz* when I was twenty-eight years old. I had never seen it before. More than anything, I thank him, member of the Wizard of Oz club, for all his input, and his understanding of the film.

I thank, and am indebted to, Carol Pearson, author of *The Hero Within*. It is her book which is the foundation of mine, and it is her ideas which springboard my own.

I wish to thank several professors at Fairhaven College where I completed my B.A. in 1988, and who each played a significant part in putting together this book.

DON McLEOD—for giving me back the wonder of fairy tale, and teaching me to see and appreciate them in new light.

DR. DANA JACK—for not only introducing me to feminine psychology, but urging me to write the "missing chapter" of Marcia's Westcott's *The Feminist Legacy*.

PAUL GLENN—artist, Jungian psychology professor, the Wizard who opened the Pandora Box of my mind.

DR. KATHRYN ANDERSON—for opening to me her private library, and for helping me, over coffee in her home, to think of the ordinary women of history who have changed our world.

GARY BORNZIN—feminist science instructor for validating and even encouraging my tendency to look at "facts" with a questioning eye, and for teaching me discipline to support my perspective.

I thank two professors at Western Washington University where I completed my M.A. in 1989.

Twelfth Night, Act III, Scene 3

DR. MEREDITH CARY—women's lit professor for resurrecting a whole new world of strong women in English literature, both characters and authors who have all been silenced by the cannon, and who, up until now, have been denied me.

LAURA KALPAKIAN—for taking such a keen interest in my work and ideas, and who, clearly, is responsible for chiseling free my style, rhythm, and voice.

I wish also to thank TURNER ENTERTAINMENT for complete and free use of extensive dialogue taken from *The Wizard of Oz.* Without their support the book would not be what it is.

I thank my neighbor CHARLIE WATSON for many things: 1) the use of her VCR and video of *The Wizard of Oz,* 2) watching my children while I wrote, 3) the long walks in the evening talking over the day's work, 4) her marvelous collection of fairy tale books, and 5) her wonderful, wonderful bean soup.

I thank my friend, SHIRLEY DOOP, a woman who plied me always with books and more books, who questioned by thesis, who gave me another perspective, and who, without a doubt, is the most challenging and supportive of my friends.

I thank my aunt, ANNE WILBEE, for being so enthusiastic, for sitting down over tea and biscuits, for going over Orphan, Pilgrim, Martyr, Warrior, and Wizard with me, and for always, always finding new things of God that gave me something to chew on.

I thank many of the men and women in my life who are living proof that dragons can be tamed:

JIM MARTINSON, double amputee, Viet Nam vet, world-class athlete and 1984 Olympian.

MIKE KING, paraplegic who made a heroic wheelchair run from Alaska to Washington, D.C. in 1985.

DOROTHY KING who has suffered so many trials and yet who remains so strong;

JUNE MASTERS BACHER, best-selling author who never lets debilitating and chronic pain stop her from doing what she does best, writing;

GLORIA CHISHOLM for her outrageous humor and sense of life;

BARBARA JOSEPH for her love; and

SANDI SHNIDER, PAT METZ, JOY JOHNSON, LISSA HALLS JOHNSON, RICH HURST, ALAN BASHAM, TOM MORTON, RICK GOUDZWAARD, LINDA WHIPPLE, and PAT HOWIE, all for their unsung, yet heroic journeys of growth.

Always I thank my children: HEATHER, PHILLIP, and BLAKE. They teach me much, and bring me much, and it is for them I always keep on.

Finally, I thank ROY M. CARLISLE of Mills House, whose intriguing and healing ideas planted new seeds of recovery in my life, whose ten minute outline—dashed off on a paper napkin over iced teas and bagels and lox in a sidewalk cafe in Berkeley—germinated the seed that eventually saw the blossoming of this book, and who three years later edited and pruned the final manuscript, making TAMING THE DRAGONS everything I wanted it to be. Mercy, *et merci.*

$\mathcal{P}$REFACE

While this book can be beneficial for both men and women, women in particular, I have always kept before me the battered psyche of the religious woman who has been mistreated by those closest to her and whose church and family have not understood the trauma she endures.

As a result, I have consistently left out the variances I might otherwise have included. For instance, in the Wizard section of this book, Part VII, I talk about self-deception. I posit that one of the reasons we deceive ourselves is because we must appear to be perfect or be considered unacceptable. I do not go into any of the other reasons why we might deceive ourselves, such as the Peter Pan syndrome, because these are not issues that concern a hurting woman. I stick to the issues that concern and affect women in pain, women who look at the world from a pain-riddled perspective. Therefore, I have not tried to write the definitive work on response to conflict, but simply a work that will address the dominant needs and concerns of women everywhere who hurt— whether they are battered, down on their luck, disillusioned, or simply going through transition.

Ten years ago there was little help for the needs of hurting women. We were told to be more grateful, to buck up, to lose weight, to shout at our mothers, to quit yelling at our children, to dress in Saran Wrap, to be more submissive, to be more aggressive, to go to work, to stay at home. Today, thanks to the pioneering work of Dr. Carol Gilligan, Marcia Wescott, Linda Kreger Silverman, Sharon Carnarton, and numerous others, we are discovering that women *are* different from men and that when we hurt we need different help than what most men need. This book, I hope, will offer you some of that different help.

I've based *Taming The Dragons* upon a book that profoundly changed my own life—*The Hero Within* by Carol Pearson. In this

book, Pearson named six behavior patterns we carry within ourselves, which, when practiced, enable us to face the mighty dragons that come part and parcel with life. She calls them archetypes;
I call them choices. I came across the book not long after it came
out in 1986, and tantalized by what she had to say, yet unable to
fully grasp it all, I chose to go back to school. I studied alternative
psychologies: feminine, family of origin, and Jungian. I studied
fairytales, too, as well as folklore, myth, and cultural story. I completed first my B.A. and then my M.A., and in the process I wore
out Pearson's book—memorizing it, studying it, and cross-
referencing it with old Bible verses I'd once memorized as a
youngster. And thus, without hardly being aware of it, *Taming The
Dragons* was begun, with Pearson's ideas frameworking my own.

Yet after taking a class in feminine psychology taught by Dr.
Dana Jack, who'd earned her Ph.D under Carol Gilligan at Harvard,
I was challenged by Dana to write out my ideas—for they came
from a religious perspective, unique to the field. *Taming The
Dragons,* at that point, became a conscious endeavor. I began by
taking Pearson's foundation, her articulation of archetypes, and
made them my own by naming and renaming. (Her Wanderer is
my Pilgrim, for example.) I then brought in my own stories—
historical, literary, and contemporary. Finally, by embracing her
conclusions, I expanded my own.

But why? Why all this trouble if there's already such a good
book on the market?

Because, as a wounded Christian woman, if I had come across
Pearson's book at the *height* of my confusion and pain, I would not
have been able to sift through her Jungian and feminist terminol-
ogy to glean her Christian truths. As it was, I had to go back to
school; not all women can do that. Also, I wrote this book because
I carry a deep concern for those caught in the same dilemmas I'd
once been in, without choice and without hope of even God,
whose Christianity can seem more brutalizing than empowering.

Taming The Dragons, then, is more pointedly "Christian"—so
that Pearson's profound and healing ideas can more easily be understood and incorporated into a religious woman's life in the
midst of her pain.

May God bless and direct and bring healing in his wings. Remember, Jesus stands at the empty tomb of our shattered hope to
ask,

"Woman, why do you weep?"

$\mathscr{H}$OW TO USE THIS BOOK

INNOCENT. If you are an ostrich with your head in the sand and ignoring the dragons of conflict raging all around you—even within you—turn to the INNOCENT section in this book to find God's challenge to sit up and take a good hard look, and to move beyond denial into redemptive work—for yourself and the world.

Acknowledging the dragon, however, can be overwhelming. The rest of the book deals with five ways to cope with the mighty dragons that seek to destroy—through the different choices of Orphan, Pilgrim, Martyr, Warrior, and Wizard.

ORPHAN. Are you feeling abandoned? Is there no safety in this dark, hard world? Is there no one you can turn to for help? Comfort? Wisdom? Turn to the "Orphan" section to find hope, the assurance that God is with you and, in the process, your own capabilities to survive.

PILGRIM. Do you need to flee, to run from danger? Are you confused? You have no answers? You don't even know the questions anymore? Turn to the "Pilgrim" section to find clarity, faith that God directs your quest, and, bottom line, who *you* are.

MARTYR. Perhaps today is one where you have to set aside your own agenda to see to the care and welfare of your children. Or maybe a neighbor needs your help. Someone has called you from the PTA to paint a prop for the fifth grade play. But you don't feel like being a doormat anymore, at the beck and call of everyone and his uncle. Turn to the "Martyr" section to find just what Jesus meant when he said "love your neighbor as yourself." He said "as" not "instead of." A Martyr learns to love herself.

WARRIOR. Or has the day turned sour, and you have to take on the role of warrior? Maybe you have to go into court to argue a speeding ticket, and you're scared. Or maybe someone on the job is undermining your work. Turn to the "Warrior" section to find God's call to war, his promise that he will go with you and, before the battle is over, your own courage.

WIZARD. Is it possible to transform conflict into something beneficial for everyone concerned? Turn to the "Wizard" section to find out how to tame evil by naming it, without and within, and then bringing into play creative alternatives. See how God transforms pain into joy—once we name our own inside dragon.

TAMING THE DRAGONS

ONE ONCE UPON A TIME...

Once upon a time . . . the raging dragon . . . a hero and a damsel in distress. Remember the old fairy tales? Prince Charming and Sleeping Beauty and happily ever after? It was always that way in our bedtime stories, right? But what about real life? Just what's happened to *our* happily ever after? Daily we live under the dragon's fire, and we can hardly even *conceive* of victory.

Once upon a time a dragon stepped across our path. The hero pulled his sword. The damsel swooned. And here we are, men slaying, women submitting, all of us forever locked into fairy-tale roles that have somehow been Christianized—thinking this is the only way to respond to conflict. And we wonder why we live in defeat.

There is defeat because, typically, men have always been taught to *conquer* conflict—to slay the dragon. Counterpoint, women have always been taught to *submit* to conflict—to subdue by swooning before the dragon, to give in.

When both of these roles, conquering and submitting, are practiced exclusively, it puts all of us at risk and backs us into a corner. For one thing, it leaves men always on the battlefield, without any R & R, and we all know that men are dying younger than women for it. Dr. Alan Basham, director of the counseling center at Seattle Pacific University in Seattle, Washington, adds another interesting angle. He believes that men

1

are dying younger than women because they are never allowed to experience the love of damsels in-distress until they *first relieve the distress*. And so men, use of sword and shield almost an art form, are dying not so much from battle wounds but from something far more deadly—they are not loved for who they are, but only for what they can *do*.

Women, on the other hand, are surviving, but in today's violent world they're surviving too often as victims, helpless damsels who cannot, dare not, pick up sword and shield in self-defense. As women we are to await the hero and in the event of the hero's ab-sence, to submit. We grow up learning to depend on rescue, and failing rescue, to then commit ourselves to martyrdom and self-sacrifice—in the hopes that if we are just "good enough," rescue will come! Like Rapunzel?

So if statistically men are dying younger than women, women statistically are surviving as victims. But if we're to defeat this destructive pattern and find victory—for *both* men and women—we need to rec-ognize roles other than those our fairy tales have as-signed.

But, is that fair? Is there not more to story than just hero and heroine, Warrior and Martyr? What of other characters and other choices when up against peril? Peter Rabbit fled. Thumbelina asked for help. Fairy godmothers guessed riddles and transformed rags into riches, frogs into princes. Warriors and Martyrs, yes, but there are also Pilgrims, Orphans, *and* Wizards!

There *is* more than one way to skin a cat, and when up against conflict there is more than one way to tame the trouble. For one thing, we can trade shoes. If we are men we can learn what it means to submit, to be a Martyr, to swoon in the face of conflict—as did Hansel at the wicked witch's house. Likewise, if we are women we can learn what it means to be the fairy-tale Warrior, to slay and conquer and defeat—as did Gretel to save Hansel. Both of us can try on new shoes altogether and learn a few new roles. What about the Pilgrim, Orphan, Wizard? It's when we insist on doing it the same old way every single time that the dragon wins—and why so many of us are not living happily ever after.

For a woman, particularly one who's been raised in the church, this concept of choice is difficult to grasp. The male Warrior and female Martyr roles are the fundamental warp and woof of our heritage; they have been for ages woven into our literature, our myths, and our laws, and then passed on down to us. So it's quite difficult to look at Scripture and see a different story, and this is why it is so difficult for us as religious women to see that we have choice. We can't help but look at the Bible and see reflected from its pages our own cultural misunderstandings.

We look into the pages of Scripture and almost automatically see only the fairy-tale roles of Warrior and Martyr. David the Warrior. Martha the Martyr. And so when the dragon roars, men rush to slay, women to submit, all of us dying and being victimized, and we zip right past all the other possible choices. We forget that there is choice. We didn't even know to look for choice.

I didn't know to look for it. Like most women raised in the church I only knew the role of Martyr. This was it as far as God was concerned; in conflict I was to swoon, to give in. But at the age of twenty-nine I was forced to wake up to the fact that this wasn't working. Self-sacrifice was getting me just that—sacrifice of self.

Why? I wondered, looking around at the failure of my life. Was I, I had to ask myself, doing everything I could? Or was I missing something important? I spent a couple of rough years poring over Scripture to find out where I had gone wrong.

At first I kept finding verses that supported the role of Martyr—good old Sarah keeping mum and winding up in the Pharaoh's harem, Martha washing dishes and serving tea and sweeping floors. These women kept shoving me back to square one. Fogged by cultural mandates I saw only men slaying and women submitting and it all seemed to work out so well in the Bible—but in real life? *Was* the sacrifice of self a woman's only option?

But then one day eating granola at my kitchen table I ran into Deborah, a Hebrew prophetess and military commander. Nobody in Sunday school had ever told me about female warriors. And then I found Abigail while eating cold toast. Nobody had ever told me about her either. She disobeyed her husband and before it was all done, David married her. Disobey her husband? And find a new life? Suddenly I began looking at men and women in the Bible with new understanding. Every morning over breakfast I was able to find, easily enough, all kinds of roles being played out in the lives of *dozens* of men and women all down through Jewish history as they battled the dragons before them! Here was Tamar, playing prostitute in order to assure herself of her lawful rights to a son by the house of Jacob! Here was Jacob "pulling the wool" (so to speak!) over his father's eyes! Suddenly, no longer stuck interpreting Scripture from my fairy-tale assigned position as Martyr, I began at last to grasp the concept of alternatives. In the face of conflict I could flee, I could fight back, I could play tricks, I could *choose!* Behold! Deborah the Warrior! Ruth the Martyr! Esther the Orphan! Hagar the Pilgrim! Abigail the Wizard! For me, a religious woman taught to blindly submit, this was liberating illumination; I rejoiced in this affirmation, this *permission* to make a different choice!

This was my beginning. I have since gone on to discover these same roles everywhere—in men and women today, in women of history, in the characters of our favorite stories. They can even be found in our fairy tales—and oftentimes more picturesque there than in the book of Judges. We don't know Deborah the Warrior, but we do know Mrs. Jumbo. Few of us have been taught to see Ruth in the role of Martyr, but

Piglet? Taking Rabbit at his word and jumping into Kanga's pocket in lieu of Roo? We certainly aren't used to looking at Wizards in the Old Testament; this idea almost seems threatening. But in fairy tales? We love and applaud our fairy godmothers.

In looking back I am not sure how any of us missed the obvious, for choice is the underlying theme both in childhood stories read to us from the cradle—and Scripture. I am not sure why the matchstick girl sticks in our minds or why we get stuck on Martha when Jesus Christ himself said Mary's way was better—for all stories—from "in the beginning" to "once upon a time"—teach us choice.

I'm not sure, and yet for some reason we have restricted ourselves, and in our self-imposed restriction the dragons win.

How then, do we choose and dragons lose?

Naming a thing brings power over it. God said, "Let us make man in our image, . . . and let them rule over the fish of the sea and the birds of the air, over the livestock, over all the earth, and over all the creatures that move along the ground."[1] And then, once man was made, he told man to name every living creature.[2] Naming empowered mankind to rule.

In the same way, by *naming* our choices we gain the power to *make* a choice. In my own life, once I got it through my head that I *could* choose, and that I had at least five options—Orphan, Pilgrim, Martyr, Warrior, and Wizard—I discovered that given any crisis I could literally sit back and decide which of the five I would use to resolve my problem. Choice took the sting out of my powerlessness. Choice enabled me to move from victim to victor. Did this particular dragon, I'd ask myself, naming my options, call for Mrs. Jumbo, the fairy-tale Warrior? Or Abigail, the Old Testament Wizard? Or was the battle one to martyr myself for, as did Ruth of Moab? As did Piglet in the Hundred-Acre Wood?

Orphan, Pilgrim, Martyr, Warrior, and Wizard. Naming is one thing, understanding another. Fortunately we have the Bible to offer example, and fairy tale to offer metaphor. Out of the Old Testament we have our beacons of choice: Esther, Hagar, Ruth, Deborah, and Abigail. We also have in *The Wizard of Oz,* handily enough in the one fairy tale: Dorothy, Scarecrow, Tinman, Lion, and Wizard. An odd combination to be sure, but one that serves a clear service.

Both Esther and Dorothy are Orphans, needing and finding help through their own courage. Hagar and the Scarecrow are Pilgrims, fleeing cultural expectations in order to seek clarity of mind and identity. Ruth and the Tinman are Martyrs, sacrificing from a position of power in order to redeem. Deborah and the Lion are Warriors, drawn into the fray to protect. And Abigail and the Wizard are Wizards, taming evil by naming it for what it really is and bringing into play creative alternatives. By following in the footsteps of these Biblical heroines and by metaphorically walking the yellow brick road of Frank Baum's Oz, we can discover on a more personal level what it means to make these choices.

Each section of this book opens "onstage" with a character from *The Wizard of Oz* that we might more easily "see" what each role is. I quickly introduce one of our women from the Bible that we might understand the scriptural support. And then because the idea of choice is so difficult for women to grasp I go on to tell nine short stories of women who have made these choices—*to bring further assurance that God has called us to creative resolution*—and to bring to light another facet of that choice. For instance, a woman Warrior may fight back with the "weapon" of a tent peg, as did Jael, or with fasting, as did Gladys Steffenson's daughter, or by simply holding back her cards, as Hezekiah should have done. A Martyr may choose to die, as did Betsie ten Boom under Nazi Germany; a Martyr may also find strength in weakness, as did Corrie ten Boom in the concentration camps. Each section then has nine of these stories: two women from history, two women from literature, two contemporary women, two more women from the Bible, and one personal example from my own life. Finally, stories told, each section concludes with a second, and closer, look at *The Wizard of Oz* and our Old Testament role models to gain further clarification as to what each role means. An Orphan *asks* for help, yes. But an Orphan also learns—in the process—how to help herself. A Wizard names evil in another person's life, true. But a Wizard also names the evil within her own life.

In the last nine years my own personal dragons have largely been those of poor health and being a single parent. Others have problems with their marriages. Still others have conflict on the job, with their kids, with their finances. Men, too, have their troubles. All of us, by the very nature of the game, are caught in conflict. Yet it seems very few of us—if we're going to be honest about it—are coping with crisis very well; we have become expert at persona. And I am convinced that for *both* men and women, we live in defeat—and from behind plastic masks—because we remain stuck responding to conflict in one prescribed way. But by *choosing* among our several options—taught to us by our fairy tales *and modeled for us in our Bibles*—we can begin to see God alongside us, and because we've *chosen* to, we can begin to put away our despair and pain, and move toward redemption and new life. And *this* is the happily ever after our fairy tales promise. Once upon a time . . . the raging dragon . . . a hero and a damsel in distress. But wait! The hero doesn't pull his sword, the damsel doesn't swoon. Both pause, and then choose—Orphan, Pilgrim, Martyr, Warrior, or Wizard. We too can choose. We too can live happily ever after.

NOTES

1. Genesis 1:26 (NIV).

2. Genesis 2:19, 20 (NIV).

TWO *I*NNOCENT

"Is there really a dragon out there?"

—*Eve the Innocent*

WE DO NOT LIVE IN THE GARDEN OF EDEN ANYMORE
Yet We Like to Pretend We Do

*Now the Lord God had planted a garden in the east, in Eden;
and there he put the man he had formed. And the Lord God
made all kinds of trees grow out of the ground—trees that
were pleasing to the eye and good for food. In the middle of
the garden were the tree of life and the tree of the knowledge
of good and evil.*

—Genesis 2:8, 9 (NIV)

Fairy tales teach us much about good and evil, and the loss of innocence. Little Red Riding Hood. Hansel and Gretel. Cinderella, and Sleeping Beauty. In the safety of story a child can come to terms with deep-seated fears: fears of abandonment, of hunger, even of death. Pulling no punches, brutal and harsh, fairy tales bring to the surface the instinctive knowledge that we're born into a wicked world full of conflict and danger.

One of the most enduring fairy tales of our day is *The Wizard of Oz.* A reason, perhaps, for its popularity is that much of it can be compared to our fall from grace—and our search for restoration in a fallen world.

When Dorothy lived with Auntie Em and Uncle Henry in Kansas she did not know the difference between good and evil, just as Adam and Eve in the Garden of Eden did not know the difference. In the fairy tale a tornado enters Kansas to snatch Dorothy out of "Eden." In the Bible a snake enters paradise to snatch Adam and Eve. In both stories everyone is plunged posthaste into a world of good versus evil.

Innocence lost, we are *all* set upon the "yellow brick road" if you will, to seek the Wizard of Oz, and Dorothy's adventures can

11

very closely be compared to ours—and Adam and Eve's—for once fallen, we need a Savior and restoration.

But like Dorothy, and Adam and Eve, we're not all that crazy about traveling the yellow brick road or facing the evil that's out there. We really only want to go home, back to Kansas, to paradise. We don't like living in a world of ruby shoes and wicked witches and hissing snakes. We want only to live in innocence forever, to live again in the Garden of Eden. But we can't, just as Eve couldn't go back to Eden and Dorothy to Kansas. Not that we don't try. Loss of innocence is a scary thing—and so we contain our fear by pretending evil doesn't exist.

We claim the role of Innocent.

This is good and appropriate if you're a child, and not enough children experience the Garden of Eden in their lives. Sadly, they are plunged too quickly into an awareness of evil and the disastrous consequences are evident all around us. But if you're an adult and still viewing life as rosy and quite the peach, it's unhealthy. Life is *not* rosy, it is *not* a peach. And none of us can keep pretending forever without inviting all kinds of trouble—for ourselves and for those around us, for we *do* live in a fallen world.

For Dorothy, a cyclone snatched her out of innocence. For Eve, a snake hissed. For us, it can be any number of mishaps. But as with both Dorothy and Eve, life does have a way of eventually forcing the issue for all of us, snatching us out of Kansas and into Oz, out of Eden into reality, out of innocence into knowledge, and this confrontation, whether we like it or not, forces us to acknowledge the reality of conflict and pain. It's not fun, and this is why so many of us dig in and *really* stick our heads in the sand.

I teach freshman composition at a state university. Eighteen years old and innocent, some of my freshmen students assume that life is easy and safe. While my job is to teach them how to write, I like to challenge them beyond their personal experience and bring to their attention a world where life isn't always so easy or safe. I introduce them to the modern-day witches of the west and the mythological dragons of the past, witches and dragons that surround all of our lives—in some way or another.

I see myself as their tornado. I catapult them from innocence into a world far different from their own, sometimes a world of oppression and poverty and corruption. I invite them to read such books as Frank Norris's *The Octopus* and Maya Angelou's *I Know*

Why the Caged Bird Sings. We learn metaphor through Dr. Martin Luther King's "Letter from a Birmingham Jail." They write reviews involving issues of the day: homelessness, gender bias, and the growing gap between the rich and poor. They write compare and contrast essays that outline the difference between their life-styles and that of Offred (Of Fred) in Margaret Atwood's *The Handmaid's Tale.* I have them do this because we, as a culture, like to pretend evil does not exist; we won't even *talk* about evil and as a result are hardly able to recognize it when it hits us upside the head—and deep inside the heart. And as with Dorothy we are left spinning, and in our spinning, the evil we pretend isn't there wins.

With some of my students I succeed in pointing out the reality of evil in our world. "You know, Teach," Pat told me in my office one day not long after writing his final paper, "I'm a redneck from Aberdeen. But when you handed me that letter Dr. Martin Luther King wrote from Birmingham's jail, I had to change my mind about a lot of things. And so if I learn nothing else in the next four years, I will still have learned something valuable. Things are not always the way I like to 'think' they are. Thanks."

With other students I fail. One day Cameron swore at me and threw onto the floor an investigative article from *People Magazine* that told of a new Underground Railroad. He, like a lot of us, didn't want to hear of women and children having to flee court orders that require children to visit fathers who sexually abuse them. Or to hear that it's the FBI hot on their frightened trail, and that it is sometimes these children's faces we see staring at us in the morning from the back of our milk cartons. We don't want to believe in a world where such things happen. We argue the statistics, we question the evidence. And sometimes, as did Cameron, we storm out of a classroom that prods too far, so desperate are we to remain innocent.

Reality infringing upon paradise is a brutal confrontation and it is so much easier to deny the reality. For my students and for many adults, the ultimate disillusionment can only be crushing. Many years ago my sister Heather was born with a congenital heart defect. My parents were able to accept the fact that evil lives and sometimes reigns, but in doing so they ran afoul of those who pretended it didn't. "Our child will not die!" insisted the parents of a little girl Heather spent hospital time with, blinding themselves to the fact that children do die, every day. Heather died when I was nine and my family went on. But the other little girl? When she died her mother's faith was destroyed. The fact is, the longer an Innocent persists in living inside the Garden and denying that life is tough beyond the gate, the more painful the fall will be. The inescapable fact is, evil does abound.

Dr. M. Scott Peck confirms this. He begins *The Road Less Traveled* with "Life is difficult."[1] Buddha taught that "life is suffering."[2] In Genesis, Adam and Eve met firsthand the "serpent" that brought about all this difficulty and suffering. Yet determined Innocents will dig in deeper, stick their heads a little deeper in the sand, systematically ignoring the serpent or dragon in order to maintain their happy illusion that life is what my friend Gloria calls "yippy-skippy." Such a position requires us to move past simple pretense to heavy-handed denial.

We, like a few of my students, will lean forward at our desks, eyes wide with disbelief. "There are not *really* 134,000 hungry children in Washington state!" we say. "There *can't* be!" Or, "But this is the nineties! Are you *sure* a woman college graduate earns the same as a male high-school dropout?" For some of us it's not even a question. We fold our arms and lean back at our desks. "*Our* government wouldn't pay just 49 percent of the poverty level to women and children on welfare! No way!" We stick out our feet. "The homeless *can't* be increasing 25 percent a year!" "The national high-school dropout rate is nowhere *near* 30 percent!"

Denial.

In other words, there are no witches or dragons to the Innocent—no matter what the evidence. There *cannot* be any dragons, because if there were, it would mean no safety. It would mean no Eden. No Kansas. It would mean we must walk the yellow brick road and take our inner journey to seek redemption, that we must *give up the role of Innocent.* And to some of my freshmen students—and to scores of us adults—it's very frightening to consider living in a world where middle-class success is not guaranteed and safety a simple matter of course.

Not long ago my fourteen-year-old daughter returned from a school trip to NASA and she brought me a bumper sticker, "MEGA-SHIT HAPPENS." Her friends were appalled that she would buy such a thing for her dear mum, but I was delighted. She did have one stipulation though. I was not to put it on the car.

There is a natural tendency to pretend that "megashit" does not "happen." We deny evil exists. Like Dorothy and Eve and all children, we long to remain the Innocent, to live forever in the Garden of Eden.

But what happens when Miss Gulch comes for Toto?

MARY

Because you have made the Lord your refuge,
  the Most High your habitation,
no evil shall befall you,
  no scourge come near your tent.

For he will give his angels charge of you
  to guard you in all your ways.
On their hands they will bear you up,
  lest you dash your foot against a stone.
You will tread on the lion and the adder,
  the young lion and the serpent you will trample under foot.
Because he cleaves to me in love, I will deliver him;
  I will protect him, because he knows my name.

  —Psalm 91:9–14 (RSV)

"I awoke shortly after midnight, and within minutes I'd been shot and my house had been burglarized. My life was turned completely upside down."

Mary[3] was asleep in bed with her three-and-a-half-year-old son when an intruder broke into her home through a bathroom window. Her husband was working the night shift as an airplane pilot.

"Because of a previous burglary attempt," she says, "I'd been praying for the ability to quickly discern good from evil." In God's answer to prayer, she awoke the night of April 15, 1989, sensing something amiss. She called 911 only moments before the intruder forced his way through her bedroom door and shot her in the face.

She remembers feeling strangely detached and overwhelmed as she folded to the floor. "I kept talking in a soft voice, saying, 'Please go away. Please go away.' "

Mary, a member of University Presbyterian Church in Seattle, Washington, does not live in the Garden of Eden, and for her, evil invaded the safety of even her own home. "I felt the struggle between good and evil," she says. "But as I lay there, watching the pool of blood grow larger and larger, I felt like God was dealing with that person, not me."

The paramedics arrived and her son, awake by now, said, "You better get a Band-Aid. My mommy has an owie on her head." Hearing his voice, Mary wondered if she'd live to see him again. "Even so," she said, "I felt really calm. I felt God was with me."

Evil lurks and even strikes, yet there is a bigger truth. God is with us. In the midst of Mary's trouble, God answered. He was there. He gave her peace. And he himself dealt with the evil raging all around. So while the Psalmist may sing "no evil shall befall you," two stanzas down he also sings, "when he calls to me, I will answer him; I will be with him in trouble."

Mary had been praying for discernment between good and evil, and before evil could strike, she woke in time to call for help. In the days that followed, the police, medics, and hospital staff, who seldom see victims survive a gunshot wound to the head, were astounded. A miracle unfolded before their eyes, for Mary lived.

And because she lived we know God is still with us, even though we don't live in the Garden of Eden anymore.[4]

LUCY

No temptation has seized you except what is common to man. And God is faithful; he will not let you be tempted beyond what you can bear. But when you are tempted, he will also provide a way out so that you can stand up under it.

—1 Corinthians 10:13 (NIV)

Sometimes we use this verse to deny the power of evil, and by doing so we let evil reign. Interpreting the word "temptation" to mean circumstances or events, rather than what it does mean— temptation to do wrong—we blind ourselves to people's burdens too heavy to bear. Assured in our minds that God will not allow too much stress to accumulate in a neighbor's life, we sit back and allow our neighbor to suffer more than he or she can withstand.

In *Uncle Tom's Cabin,* the novel that sparked the Civil War by exposing the evils of slavery, Tom watched a Christian woman kill herself in despair.

Mr. Haley was the slave trader. At one spot along the Mississippi, while taking his "gang" south to sell, he stopped off and Tom watched him reboard with a black woman traipsing along after him, chirruping happily to her ten-month-old baby. She was, it was duly explained, on her way down to Louisville to be hired out to work in the same tavern as her husband. But Haley interrupted; he'd bought her and was going to sell her South.

So instead of going to live with her husband, she would never see him again. At Louisville, the distraught Lucy tucked her sleeping baby into a corner and ran to the front rails of the boat in hopes of catching a last glimpse of a husband she'd never see again. While her back was turned, Haley sold her baby for forty-five dollars to a man who slipped away unseen.

Harriet Beecher Stowe pounced on the Northern reader for turning a blind eye to such evil. "The trader," she wrote, "had arrived at that stage of Christian . . . perfection which has been recommended by some preachers . . . of the north . . . in which he had completely overcome every humane weakness and prejudice. His heart was exactly where yours, sir, and mine could be brought, with proper effort and cultivation. The wild look of anguish and utter despair that the woman cast upon him might have disturbed one less practised; but he was used to it. He had seen that same look hundreds of times. You can get used to such things, too, my friend . . . . "⁵

Tom tried to comfort Lucy, to tell her of a caring Jesus. But, says Stowe, "the ear was deaf with anguish."

"O! what shall I do?" Lucy moaned in the black of night. "O Lord! O good Lord, do help me!" At midnight Tom awoke, felt a stir of air, then a brush past his shoulder. In the silence of the night he heard the splash, and when he looked, Lucy's place on the deck was empty.

Today we don't have slavery. We have El Salvador and fugitives fleeing an unsympathetic U.S. for the Canadian border. We have women and children as the fastest growing poor in a country which is the wealthiest in the world. We have sexual discrimination, gender bias, and whole cities where crime, violence, and despair are as common as safety, peace, and hope are to the white, middle-class American.

But like the Northerners of 1852, and like Haley the slave trader, we've grown so used to the face of evil "out there, down there" that the anguish no longer means anything to us. Evil runs rampant, and people—even Christians like Lucy—kill themselves (or go crazy, or get sick, or live emotionally paralyzed lives) from the despair of it all.

Sometimes the burden *is* too great to bear, and like the Northerners, we can't rest in religious triteness, because for others "the ear is deaf with anguish." We need to wake up because none of us live in the Garden of Eden anymore.

CHRISTINE

So now, since we have been made right in God's sight by faith in his promises, we can have real peace with him because of what Jesus Christ our Lord has done for us.

For because of our faith, he has brought us into this place of highest privilege where we now stand, and we confidently and joyfully look forward to actually becoming all that God has had in mind for us to be.

We can rejoice, too, when we run into problems and trials for we know that they are good for us—they help us learn to be patient.

And patience develops strength of character in us and helps us trust God more each time we use it until finally our hope and faith are strong and steady. Then, when that happens, we are able to hold our heads high no matter what happens and know that all is well, for we know how dearly God loves us, and we feel this warm love everywhere within us because God has given us the Holy Spirit to fill our hearts with his love.

—Romans 5:1–5 (LB)

My cousins were almost home, pushing their bikes up the last of the hill. It was a winter evening early in the new year 1974, and a slight drizzle hurried them along; Patty was thirteen, Christine eleven. Lights from the kitchen window could be seen through the trees. They were nearly home.

Suddenly, a car driven by a young man blinded by the setting sun came gunning up over the ridge. Patty ran the half block home screaming. Uncle Stan, the town doctor, was paged. Christine had been in an accident.

Seventeen hundred miles away, and a few days later, I came home late from work. A letter from my folks was in the mailbox. "I'm sorry to be the one to break the news," my mother wrote, "but Christine was killed today while riding her bike home for supper."

Christine? I let the letter fall to the floor, my eyes automatically sliding to the wall where I'd hung a small hooked rug Christine and I had made together a few summers before. It was all I had of the sweet little cousin I loved. "Oh, Christine," I wept, tears rushing to my eyes the moment I buried my face into the dusty wool. "Oh, Christine . . . Oh, God . . ." And then suddenly the evil of her death choked me in pain—for she was dead. Dead! Dead! I beat my fists against the rug and screamed my agony into her careful work. "Oh, Christine!" Dead, dead because—because why? Dead because of a careless driver? Needless, pointless death! Had evil won?

I was inconsolable for days.

Then came a second letter from my mother. "Uncle Stan," she wrote, "went into Christine's room after everything was over and sat down at the new little table he'd gotten her for Christmas. Her Bible was open. She'd been reading it before going off to school that morning, and she'd underlined the first five verses of Romans 5."

So now, since we have been made right in God's sight by faith in his promises, we can have real peace with him because of what Jesus Christ our Lord has done for us . . .

Christine spoke from heaven. Evil receded.

(LB) . . . we are able to hold our heads high no matter what happens and know that all is well, for we know how dearly God loves us . . .

Evil slid back further, finally to vanish in the victory of God's ultimate promise. We are not without hope, even though none of us live in the Garden of Eden anymore.

ALTHALIAH

Everyone must submit himself to the governing authorities, for there is no authority except that which God has established. The authorities that exist have been established by God. Consequently, he who rebels against the authority is rebelling against what God has instituted, and those who do so will bring judgment on themselves. For rulers hold no terror for those who do right, but for those who do wrong.

—Romans 13:1–3 (NIV)

If evil ran in Jezebel's veins, it ran even deeper in her daughter's. Athaliah ascended the throne by slaughtering her own grandchildren to become Judah's only reigning queen.

She married Jehoram, eldest son of Jehoshaphat, king of Judah, and when he took the throne she brought with her Baal, her mother's god from Israel. Jehoram's brothers, however, resisted her influence, determined to remain loyal to both Jehovah and the people of Judah. For their defiance King Jehoram had them murdered.

Elijah had fought Jezebel; now he fought Athaliah. He prophesied that a wretched disease would kill her husband, and in eight years Jehoram died as prophesied. Ahaziah, Jehoram and Athaliah's son, took over and she moved into greater power than ever before as queen mother.

Within a year, however, her son too was dead, and Athaliah, momentum behind her, moved into high gear. She seized the throne and set out to destroy "all the seed royal," her own blood relations and grandchildren, and for six years her reign was supreme.

Unbeknownst to her, however, her stepdaughter Jehosheba had rescued one of the royal babies from the bloody massacre and had been raising him in secrecy. When he turned seven years old, the high priest brought him out of hiding and with the help of the Levites crowned him king.

At the tumultuous cry of freedom, Queen Athalia went to investigate. There in the Temple she'd desecrated for Baal the new king stood, surrounded by princes with their trumpets. All the people of the land were rejoicing, sounding their own trumpets and singing with instruments of music.[6]

"Treason! *Treason!*" screamed Athaliah.

"Slay her not," said the high priest, "in the house of the Lord."

She was slain at the horse gate by the palace, and her body was left in the path of trampling hooves, a death very much like her mother's.

I can't help but wonder why the apostle Paul wrote in Romans that all authority is ordained of God, that all rulers hold no terror for those who do good, but only for those who do evil, and that to resist authority is to resist God. How can this be when Elijah dared to alternately confront and flee the wicked Jezebel? And Jehosheba dared to defy Athaliah and rescue Joash to raise in secrecy? And where would any of us be if there hadn't been people like Harriet Tubman, Elizabeth Cady Stanton, Dr. Martin Luther King, and others, Elijahs and Jehoshebas who dared to stand up and pronounce evil for what it was? History, if it tells us anything, tells us that none of us live in the Garden of Eden anymore.

WENDY

If anyone has material possessions and sees his brother in need but has no pity on him, how can the love of God be in him? Dear children, let us not love with words or tongue but with actions and in truth.

—1 John 3:17, 18 (NIV)

If anyone does not provide for his relatives, and especially for his immediate family, he has denied the faith and is worse than an unbeliever.

—1 Timothy 5:8 (NIV)

Sometime during the last presidential campaign eight-year-old Wendy Jacob was sitting on the couch doing her Bible reading. There was a sudden, "Uh-oh."

"What's the matter, Wendy?" her mother asked, for her face was pained.

"This verse. Poor daddy." And she read aloud 1 Timothy 5:8. There was nothing her mother could say. Just the week before Wendy had brought home one of her papers from school, framed in black.

> If I could ask the presidential candidate one question, I would ask: "What would you do about child abuse?" I think this is very important because some fathers don't pay as much child support as they're supposed to. If the fathers don't pay they're [sic] child support, the women don't have much money, and if the women don't have much money, they can't buy much food, so they're hungry at lot of the time!
>
> From Wendy, Grade 3

Not long ago a friend of my daughter's came over to the house and I teased him about something. He stiffened, his eyes went frantic, darting back and forth, and my heart stopped. Something was wrong. Later, I was not surprised to find that Jeff's stepfather, a member of the local church, terrorizes his seventeen-year-old stepson with verbal abuse and ridicule. Too, Jeff is required to be home at all times to babysit five younger brothers and sisters while his parents work. Simultaneously his father asks, "Why don't you run away from home?" We-need-you-we-don't-need-you is the message Jeff gets every day of his life and anyone who stops to look can see the confusion in his eyes.

Scott Peck points out that evil is often subtle. Evil resides in the mother of three next door and the deacon in the church down the street.[7] "It is not their sins per se," he writes, "that characterize evil people, rather it is the *subtlety and persistence and consistency* of their sins." Sin is not so much the evil as it is *"the refusal to acknowledge it."*[8] And left unacknowledged, evil numbs our conscience.

Which is why James and Phyllis Alsdurf, authors of *Battered into Submission,* can write that "one can conservatively estimate that for every 60 married women in a church, 10 suffer emotional and verbal abuse, and 2 or 3 will be physically abused by their husbands."[9] And why Esther Lee Olson and Ken Petersen in *No Place to Hide* can quote a more familiar but unbelievable study that reveals that as many as one out of every two wives in America will experience abuse by their husbands.[10] Paul Tournier himself admits to brutal violence—in word, thought, and deed.[11]

No, evil is not always Jezebel or a man who shoots you in the face, but a father who, when his children ask for bread, gives them, in the name of God, stones. A husband who, while he says he loves, beats. We may not see the evil in and around us, but, sadly, too many women and children know and understand that none of us live in the Garden of Eden anymore.

$\mathcal{A}$CKNOWLEDGMENT OF EVIL INVITES BLAME

Yet We Must Get Past Blame and Instead Choose to Resolve

Then the man and his wife heard the sound of the Lord God as he was walking in the cool of the day, and they hid from the Lord God among the trees of the garden. But the Lord God called to the man, "Where are you?"

He answered, "I heard you in the garden, and I was afraid because I was naked; so I hid."

And he said, "Who told you that you were naked? Have you eaten from the tree that I commanded you not to eat from?"

The man said, "The woman you put here with me—she gave me some fruit from the tree, and I ate it."

Then the Lord God said to the woman, "What is this you have done?"

The woman said, "The serpent deceived me, and I ate."

—Genesis 3:8–13 (NIV)

M iss Gulch is on her way. Toto is doomed. And denial of dragons will only get us so far before the music comes on, ominous and galloping.

"Ooh, I hate this part!" squeals Blake, nine years old, as we watch the dragon lady ride her bicycle grimly down the dusty Kansas road, mouth prim. We see Uncle Henry let her in at the front gate, letting it snap shut against her bottom.

"I'm taking that dog," Miss Gulch minces tartly, "to the sheriff and make sure he's destroyed!"

"Destroyed? Toto?" breathes out Dorothy, frantically clutching her little dog in her arms. "Oh, you can't, you mustn't! Uncle Henry, you won't let her, will you? Please, Auntie Em, Toto didn't mean to, he didn't know he was doing anything wrong. I'm the one who ought to be punished! I'm the one who let him go in her garden! You can send me to bed without supper!"

Loss of innocence, moving out of childhood at the nudge of evil, is a painful process. Dorothy, racing home with Toto in her arms, was overwhelmed by the infringement of her safety. In her panic and unable to deny the dragon facing her—Miss Gulch—Dorothy latched onto the first line of defense, the same one we all reach for—blame. In her case, self-blame.

Blame works two ways, like a double-edged sword: we can project it onto someone else or we can internalize it. One summer I'd taken my children to the beach and a seven-year-old boy drowned. We all had to help look for him. The experience was traumatic for me, but when I went to a friend for comfort his response was a stinging blow.

"What's the matter with you?" he wanted to know. "It's not like it was one of our kids! *And where was the mother?*"

It wasn't until years later I saw that my friend was merely responding out of the precarious position of the Innocent. Rather than acknowledge that dragons do sweep down from time to time and snatch away children (his children! my children!), he had to pretend that death could only happen to careless people who didn't watch their kids properly. My friend *had* to criticize the heartbroken mother for not being more watchful so that he (I later saw) could maintain the illusion that the world was safe—for him, for me. Because he, after all, was a good father and I, after all, was a good mother.

My reaction, on the other hand, was to internalize the blame rather than project it. If only I had understood the danger faster! I'd agonized, shifting the blame inward. If only I'd gone out quicker to look. If only I hadn't had my children with me. If only I had been on the ball the tragedy would not have happened! If only . . . if only . . . if only. For me, too, there was no dragon— there was only inept me. *Because it was far easier to accept an inept me than to contend with a ferocious dragon that snatched children indiscriminately from a summer beach!*

We do this, I think, to bring a measure of control to dragons we can no longer deny. By blaming either ourselves, someone else, or even God, there is an unspoken belief that if we would just do it "right," we could alleviate future crisis. There really is no dragon; there is only our own foolishness, our own stupidity, our own ignorance, our own ill luck. Or, if we're like Lucy in *Peanuts,* there is always Charlie Brown. Assigning blame, be it projected *or* internalized, is a stab in the dark when the dragons get too big to ignore.

When Dorothy is confronted with the dragon of Miss Gulch, she tries to maintain her safety by internalizing the blame—she says it was all her fault. Send *her* to bed without supper. Blame, be it projected or internalized, is an attempt to keep the undeniable dragons at bay—and out of our paradise, our safe utopia.

But it didn't work for Dorothy in Kansas, it certainly didn't work for Eve in the Garden of Eden, and it doesn't work for us today. And if we persist, we suffer for it.

John Westfall, one of my pastors, has often said that there are two kinds of people in life: those who are responsible and those who are not. Dr. M. Scott Peck says that most people who visit a psychiatrist are suffering from what is called either a "neurosis" or a "character disorder," and while those terms sound like labels left best for *One Flew Over the Cuckoo's Nest,* they're just John's ideas gussied up. "The neurotic," Peck explains, "assumes too much responsibility; the person with a character disorder not enough."[12] And when neurotics are in conflict with the world (confronting the dragon), Peck goes on to explain, they automatically assume the blame—because they see themselves as responsible. Those with character disorders, says Peck, when they are in conflict with the world (confronting the dragon), automatically assume that the world is at fault.[13] Either way you cast the blame, though, the dragon wins.

Let's suppose Dorothy blamed Miss Gulch instead of herself. Would it have changed the fact that there was a sheriff's warrant for the seizure of Toto? No. So whether Dorothy or Miss Gulch is at fault is immaterial and hardly the question. The conflict is that *Toto is being stuffed into a basket and hauled off to his doom!* And those of us who refuse to acknowledge evil can only do what Dorothy did, helplessly stare at Auntie Em and Uncle Henry and then run crying into our bedroom.

Some of us get stuck here, in deep pain. As an adult Innocent we're not sure what hit us—but we feel some measure of safety because we at least know who's fault all this is, right? A battered woman (Peck's neurotic type, John's responsible type) will *never* accuse her husband of evil. Instead she'll agree "with society's belief that the batterer would change his behavior if only she could change her behavior."[14] This is her measure of safety. *He* won't hurt me again if *I* do it right, she reasons.

A batterer, however (Peck's character disorder type, John's irresponsible type), will *always* blame his victim, because it is *her* fault. "The batterer feels justified in his violent behavior because society says it is really the woman's fault, not his."[15] This is his measure of safety. *I* won't hurt her again if *she* does it right, he thinks.

But in a world where countless women are beaten by their husbands,[16] we would have to say blame doesn't stop the dragon at all—just as asking to be sent to bed without supper did not stop Miss Gulch from taking Toto.

Let's leave our fairy tale behind and turn to the Bible.

In Genesis we see Adam blaming Eve and Eve blaming the snake, and rather than interpret the passage in light of personal responsibility, we often see it as an admonishment not to project, but to internalize blame. But blame, whether it be projected or internalized, *never* works. The point of the passage is not to decry one method over another—*but to move us past blame altogether and into the realm of personal responsibility.*

What counts is that something is wrong in paradise. There is a serpent, a snake in the grass, a dragon. And because there is a problem, we have to give up assigning blame and move forward, embracing personal responsibility—which means we have to act. "Now what?" is the question to ask, not "Whose fault is this?"

It *has* to be a question of personal responsibility; there is no other way. For Dorothy, it's a question of getting Toto back. For us it's a question of facing our conflict and then resolving it.

Dragons don't go away just because we stick our heads in the sand and act like ostriches. They go away only when we choose to give up our innocence and take responsibility for resolution—and then spread our wings to meet the dragons.

Scott Peck says that no problem can be solved until an individual assumes the responsibility for solving it.[17] And in *The Wizard of Oz* isn't this just what Dorothy does? After Toto clambers back in through the window she scoops him up and says, "We'll run away! I'm not going to let anyone take you away from me!"

Without realizing it, she chooses personal responsibility and thereby leaves behind forever the role of Innocent. No longer can she live in the Garden of Eden, denying and blaming. Innocence lost, she has to grow up: she knows the difference between good and evil now, and it has become *her* responsibility to combat the dragon, to save Toto. She responds, almost simultaneously, by choosing the roles of Orphan, Pilgrim, Martyr, and Warrior.

"Oh, what are we going to do?" she wails, feeling the sudden helplessness of the Orphan. But she quickly becomes the Warrior and packs a basket. She takes off, a Pilgrim. "Can I join you in your travels?" she asks Professor Marvel when she runs into him, "to see the crown heads of Europe?" But when Professor Marvel plays on her sense of responsibility by telling her that Auntie Em is ill, she then takes on the role of Martyr and sets off for home. The only role Dorothy does not follow is that of Wizard, usually the last and most difficult role to understand.

But because she dared to face the dragon—leaving behind first denial and then blame—and because she took that first step beyond the role of Innocent into personal responsibility, she found herself caught up in a whirlwind that hastened her forward on a journey toward victory. Life, when we at last confront the dragon, will always move us speedily forward, propelling us out of Eden and toward restoration and redemption.

Which is why it's so frightening. We sense the cyclone. We see the dizzy, buffeting darkness of the unknown. Like Dorothy, we feel the terrifying surge of danger and awesome weight of responsibility for what is wrong in our lives. We drag our heels, wanting only to be safe. We'd really rather live neurotically in our Garden of Eden, full of denial and blame. But the black clouds descend. "Auntie Em!" we scream while the tornado advances. We kick on the cellar door, wind tearing now at our skirts. "Uncle Henry! Oh, Auntie Em! Let me in! It's me! Dorothy!"

But we've been cast out of Eden, and there's no way back.

Or is there?

Carol Pearson points out in *The Hero Within* that the irony here is that we do return to Eden. "We can and do return to love and abundance," she says, "but only as a result of taking our journeys."[18]

Dorothy, her long journey over, does return to Kansas, and although we know Miss Gulch awaits her, we can rest assured that Dorothy has learned her own strength. In Oz she acquires the inner knowledge that while she is no longer an Innocent, she is everything else. She is Orphan, Pilgrim, Martyr, Warrior, and even Wizard. She knows how to confront evil and come out on top.

The same is true for us. It's not until we embrace the unknown and assume responsibility for the evil we meet instead of looking for someone (including ourselves) to blame, not until we go to "Oz" and take our own journey that we will ever be able to discover our inner power, God's strength, and be able to walk with grace in our fallen world.

Scary, yes. But we cannot pretend to live in Eden anymore. Toto has come through the window, and it is up to us.

NOTES

1. M. Scott Peck, *The Road Less Traveled* (New York: Simon & Schuster, 1978), 1.

2. Peck, *The Road Less Traveled,* 1.

3. Last name deleted by request.

4. Adapted from Eva S. Nixon, "Mary Counts Miracles in Her Night of Terror," *UPC Times,* vol. 9, no. 4 (July 1989): 1, 6.

5. Harriet Beecher Stowe, *Uncle Tom's Cabin, or Life Among the Lowly* (Boston: John P. Jewett, 1852). Chapter 12.

6. 2 Chronicles 23:13 (NIV).

7. M. Scott Peck, *People of the Lie* (New York: Simon & Schuster, 1983), 47.

8. Peck, *People of the Lie,* 69 [emphasis mine].

9. James and Phyllis Alsdurf, *Battered into Submission,* quoted in "Battered into Submission," *Christianity Today,* 16 June 1989, 24.

10. Esther Lee Olson and Ken Petersen, *No Place To Hide* (Wheaton, IL: Tyndale, 1985), 9.

11. Alsdurf, *Christianity Today,* 25.

12. Peck, *The Road Less Traveled,* 35.

13. Peck, *The Road Less Traveled,* 35.

14. Lenore E. Walker, *The Battered Woman* (New York: Harper & Row, 1979), 33.

15. Walker, *The Battered Woman,* 15.

16. Olson and Petersen, *No Place To Hide,* 9.

17. Peck, *The Road Less Traveled,* 32.

18. Carol Pearson, *The Hero Within* (San Francisco: Harper & Row, 1986), 26.

THREE $\mathcal{O}$RPHAN

"Someone please rescue me from this dragon."

—*Ruth the Orphan*

$\mathscr{D}$RAGONS OVERWHELM
But There Is Always a Hero To Help

Now there was in the citadel of Susa a Jew ... named
Mordecai ... who had been carried into exile from Jerusalem
by Nebuchadnezzar king of Babylon. ... Mordecai had a
cousin named Hadassah, whom he had brought up because she
had neither father nor mother.

—Esther 2:5–7 (NIV)

I t is up to us to save Toto, but how? How do we move from
denial of dragons to confronting them and resolving the conflict?

It's tough because crisis moves us directly from Innocent to
Orphan, immobilizing us. We thought we had only Miss Gulch to
contend with, but now there's a dead witch under the house, and
another witch is wanting to know who killed her, and there's a
good witch too! *A good witch?* And the wicked witch says we
killed her sister. But we didn't mean to kill anyone! "I'll get you,
my pretty," the wicked Witch of the West screams in our face,
"*and* your little dog too!" If Toto was in danger before, he really
is now—*and so are we.*

Crisis wakes us up to the fact that none of us live in the Garden
of Eden anymore, but it also shatters our innocence and leaves us
disillusioned, abandoned, and often painfully confused and in need
of help. Death. Divorce. Unemployment. Failing health. Wayward
children. The brutal slaying of a seven-year-old in the park just last
week. No, this is not paradise where we live, but a fallen world,
and we see the dragons clearly enough now. But where is the
hero? "Oh, I'd give anything to be out of Oz," says Dorothy. "But
how?" How do we get out of this mess? *Oh, God,* we all wail, *why
is this happening to me?*

The Orphan is consumed by fear and insecurity. Overwhelmed by dragons we once denied, we distrust our capabilities and are easily convinced we can't make it on our own. "Someone please rescue me," we plead. "I don't know how to take care of myself!" And half the time, we don't.

"Brenda," my sister used to ask right after my divorce, "what can I do?"

"I don't know," I'd weep, "*just please help me!*"

Dorothy asked the good witch Glinda, "Will you help me? *Can you help me? How do I get out of Oz?*"

Way back in 883 B.C., Esther, queen of Xerxes, asked the same thing. "But Mordecai," she said, catapulted into her own terrifying land of Oz, "all the king's servants and the people of the king's province know that if any man or woman goes to the king inside the inner court without being called, there is but one law! All alike are to be put to death, except the one to whom the king holds out the golden scepter that he may live! And I," she pleaded, when Mordecai insisted she entreat the king to save the Jews, "have not been called to come in to the king these thirty days!"[1] *How, Mordecai, am I going to do this?*

Innocent to Orphan, we spiral from denial to the need for rescue and our bedtime fairy tales teach us this well enough. "Oh, Grandmother, what big teeth you have . . ." The wolf leaps. Teeth snap. Crisis tears at our throat and we are consumed.

So much for confronting dragons.

Therapist Tresa Wiggins says that the number-one task facing the Orphan is learning self-reliance, for then the tough business of confronting dragons can begin. "The Orphan's primary task," she says, "is to learn she isn't as helpless as she may feel. Dorothy," Wiggins explains, "could have returned to Kansas at any time. *You've always had the power to go back to Kansas*—that's what the good witch Glinda told Dorothy. So Dorothy was never without power; she just didn't know she could take care of herself. The journey was to teach her."[2]

M. Scott Peck would agree. "Problems," he says, "call forth our courage and our wisdom."[3] This is what the inner journey, the yellow brick road, is all about: self-discovery and finding redemption. The good witch Glinda, however, did not tell any of this to

Dorothy at the beginning of her journey, for there is no use in telling Orphans to snap to and be self-reliant when they don't think they can. Orphans first need the promise of a hero, of hope. Orphans need to know, says Carol Pearson in *The Hero Within,* "that they *will* be cared for."[4] That way they can break past their fear long enough to get moving again.

Which is exactly what the good witch Glinda gives Dorothy at the onset of her journey—no lectures, just hope of rescue. She gives Dorothy the promise of a wizard who might help her get back to Kansas.

"He lives in the Emerald City," she said, "and that's a long journey from here. Did you bring your broomstick with you?"

"No, I'm afraid I didn't."

Hope doesn't necessarily mean rescue will be easy or that it will be handed over on a silver platter or with the wave of a magic wand. We're not given everything that will speed us on our way. Dorothy would have to walk. We are, however, given what we need. "Never," says the good witch, "let those ruby slippers off your feet for a moment, or you will be at the mercy of the wicked Witch of the West."

Ruby slippers. In the ancient world shoes symbolized liberty,[5] and fairy tales often make use of this. In *The Wizard of Oz* the ruby shoes guaranteed Dorothy a measure of safety in the midst of chaos so she could seek the hero she was promised.

"How do I start for the Emerald City?" she asks, ruby shoes on her feet.

"It's always best to start at the beginning. All you do is follow the yellow brick road."

"But, what happens if—"

And here is the rub. Hope is one thing, trust quite another, and Dorothy hesitates. In the midst of crisis how do we know *who* to trust? For the Orphan, traumatized by crisis, it can be very confusing. Who is right? Who is wrong? *Is* there such a thing as a good witch? How can we trust when crisis has turned the whole world upside down? And whatever happened to those easy days when everything was so black and white?

"Follow the yellow brick road," the good witch encourages and before Dorothy can decide, the good witch disappears, leaving her the freedom to choose. Herein lies a rule of thumb. Bad witches demand. Good witches, however, leave the choice up to us. Dragons insist, hovering to make sure we comply, but God always, always allows us the freedom to decide.

Dorothy had to decide. She could go back to her house and wait for rescue that might never come. She could stay with the Munchkins and hope for the best, living for years in fear of the wicked Witch of the West. Or she could strike out alone, trusting the good witch, the ruby shoes, and the yellow brick road to take her to the Wizard—and home again. Granted, the choices weren't all that terrific. Each carried risk; witches and dragons lurked. Scott Peck reminds us that "frequently our choices lie between the lesser of two evils, but it is still within our power," he says, "to make these choices."[6] And for the Orphan, there has to be this fundamental choice—to trust and move forward on our own or to give up in our helplessness and retreat, and if we do the latter not even God can help us. Dorothy, however, puts the toe of her ruby shoe to the start of the yellow brick road.

"Just follow the yellow brick road," she whispers, her mind made up.

Queen Esther had to make the same choice. Like the good witch who gave promise of a wizard, Mordecai encouraged his cousin by saying, "Who knows, Esther, whether you have not come to the kingdom for such a time as this?" He gave indirect hope (and for some of us, this is all we get) that God perhaps had a bigger plan that would accommodate her peril. For Esther it was enough.

"All right," she said. "Go, and gather all the Jews in Susa, and fast for me. Do not eat or drink for three days and nights. I and my maids will do the same, and when this is done, I will go to the king though it is against the law. And if I perish, I perish."[7]

It was not an easy step for Esther to take," says Wiggins, "for it involved a tremendous leap of faith. But then, it's the same leap of faith we all have to make. And it's this leap—and the fact that we *do* survive—that begin to teach us self-reliance."

So simple, yet so hard.

Esther had the prayers of her people to see her through. Dorothy had her ruby shoes. What do we have to assure us that there is hope for rescue?

"Faith comes from what is heard," writes the apostle Paul, "and what is heard comes by the preaching of Christ."[8] We have the Word of God.

But it's our choice whether we listen or not.

"Just follow the yellow brick road," Dorothy chants. "Just follow the yellow brick road." But she's going in circles, getting nowhere in a hurry. The Munchkins rush in with support. "Just follow the yellow brick road," sing-songs the mayor, bowing from the waist. "Just follow the yellow brick road," says another, stepping out of the way. As the circle unwinds, the munchkins rush to see her to the border of Munchkinland, where they all break into a skip and a song. "We're off to see the Wizard, the wonderful Wizard of Oz. We're off, we're off, we're off, we're off . . . ." The note hangs, Dorothy does a two-step, and we, if *we* want, can open our Bibles and set off on our own journey too. We, too, have a wizard, a hero, to seek.

The Orphan asks, "Where is the hero?"

The answer lies both within *and* beyond, and once we choose to make that leap of faith we'll find it. Somewhere, somehow. And this is how the Orphan confronts an overwhelming dragon—blind trust in a hero we don't yet see.

GLORIA

*. . . O you of little faith? So do not worry, saying, "What shall
we eat?" or "What shall we drink?" or "What shall we wear?"
For the pagans run after all these things, and your heavenly
Father knows that you need them. But seek first his kingdom
and his righteousness, and all these things will be given to you
as well. Therefore do not worry about tomorrow, for tomorrow
will worry about itself. Each day has enough trouble of its
own.*

—*Matthew 6:30b–34 (NIV)*

Gloria Chisholm has five kids. A couple of years ago the landlord sold the house she was living in, forcing her out. Who,
we wondered, in their right mind would rent her a house now?
She worked as an editor for a religious publishing house. As far
as the rest of us were concerned, she was doomed, God or no
God.

She looked for weeks. There were no apartments. They just
don't make them that big anymore. And the houses that were big
enough? The owners would see her coming, brood in tow, and
before they could get to the front door the owners would be out
the back.

D-day was around the corner, and we were all getting a bit
worried. Finally we hit upon a plan. After her kids had had a hard
day at play and looked the part, Gloria was going to borrow a
neighbor's dog and then pile the whole kit and caboodle into the
van and take them down to the busiest corner of Lynnwood, Washington, during rush-hour traffic. There they would hang out, pac-
ing up and down the curb, big signs bobbing about their necks,
knobby knees peeking out below, borrowed dog chained to the
fire hydrant. HELP! MOTHER OF FIVE NEEDS HOME BY TOMOR-
ROW NIGHT! BAG LADY WITH KIDS NEEDS HOUSE! HELP! I was
going to call up Nick Walker of Seattle's four o'clock news on
KIRO TV. This was going to be a "human interest" feature that
would attract the interest of even Ronald Reagan.

We were all set to go. Saturday she had to be out. Friday afternoon and we were going to wake up the town.

But then Gloria got a phone call. Turned out, a house just a mile away was up for rent. Same price, more room, and the kids could go to the same school.

"Ah, darn," Gloria grumbled, truly put out. "Isn't it awful how God takes care of everything so nicely? Now we can't have all that fun!"

We had fun anyway, moving her into the five-bedroom house complete with two kitchens and a den, because now we knew for sure that none of us are ever without help.

BRENDA

> . . . Jacob sent word to Rachel and Leah to come out to the fields where his flocks were. He said to them, "I see that your father's attitude toward me is not what it was before, but the God of my father has been with me. You know that I've worked for your father with all my strength, yet your father has cheated me by changing my wages ten times. However, God has not allowed him to harm me."
>
> —Genesis 31:4–7 (NIV)

As a single mother I can relate to Jacob and his feelings of being cheated. In eight years my child support has been changed thirty-eight times. I live in constant economic upheaval and so understand exactly how Jacob felt.

There are other ways to be cheated, too. We can be cheated out of recognition, time, honor, even love. In the business world we can be cheated when someone takes credit for something we did. Gossip robs us of our reputation. A busy boss may fail to be appreciative. Employees fudge on their time slips. Beyond the workplace there are even more ways to be cheated. Everyone has horror stories of car mechanics, attorneys, and politicians. And yet God did not allow Laban to harm Jacob.

I remember one early spring day going out to my mailbox to look for a very late child support check. I was upset and even angry. Laban, it seemed, held all the cards.

Then I opened my box and there was the front cover to my very first book. I remember looking at it, the sun warm on my cheek, reflecting off the glossy print; I saw my own name in big, bold type along the bottom. *He can't hurt me anymore.* The thought came out of nowhere and I stood stunned by the force of it. When I went back to the house the thought tumbled around and around inside my head. *He can't hurt me anymore. He can't hurt me anymore.*

I plugged in the tea kettle, realizing for the first time just how great, how dreadfully deep, how black and immense my fear as a single mother really was. I'd been living in the shadow of starvation and with the fear of homelessness, worry for my children's welfare always driving me to work harder, save more, juggle, skimp, go without. But as I stood waiting for the water to boil, the only thought racing through my mind was, "He can't hurt me anymore," racing and racing and picking up speed until goose bumps stood up on my arms and I sat down at the kitchen table and cried in relief.

Unlike Jacob, I didn't have a Rachel to talk to, or even a Leah. But I had God talking to me. "I will allow him to cheat," God whispered gently in the warmth of that early spring afternoon while bees hummed at the window sill and the scent of new growth from the garden outside mingled with the dust motes, "but, Brenda, I will never let him harm you. Ever."

There is relief in knowing that while God does allow others to cheat us, he will never allow them to harm us. Gossip, lack of understanding, unnecessary car parts, empty promises—we can feel abandoned and orphaned, unheard from and insignificant in the great big world. But God whispers, the tea kettle whistles, and we know that we are safe, because none of us are ever without help.

SOJOURNER TRUTH

Do not take advantage of a widow or an orphan. If you do and they cry unto me, I will certainly hear their cry. My anger will be aroused, and I will kill you with the sword . . .

—Exodus 22:22–24 (NIV)

Sojourner Truth was born a slave in 1797 in Hurley, New York. It was against the law to sell a slave South, yet when Dr. Gedney sold Sojourner's five-year-old son Peter to his brother Solomon, it did not stop Solomon from selling the little boy to an Alabama planter named Fowler.

Outraged and grief-stricken, Sojourner Truth walked all the way to New Paltz to find Solomon, and when she got no satisfaction from him, came back to Mrs. Gedney. "Ugh!" said Mrs. Gedney. "A fine fuss to make about a little nigger! Why, haven't you as many of them as you can see to and take care of? Making such a hallooballoo about the neighborhood, and all for a paltry nigger!"

"I knew I'd have him again," said Sojourner Truth. "I was sure God would help me to get him. Why, I felt so tall within—I felt as if the power of a nation was with me."[9]

And she did have him with her again. Relying on God and her own rugged, daring determination, in 1828 she, a single, black slave woman, took a white man, Solomon Gedney, to court for selling her son South—and won.

But when she got Peter back he was covered from head to foot with the scars of brutal beatings. Peter, trying to ease his mother's fury, whispered, "This is nothing, Mammy. If you would see Phillis, I guess you'd scare. She had a little baby, and Fowler cut her till the milk as well as blood ran down her body. You would scare to see Phillis, Mammy." Sojourner Truth, unable to stop the rage, cursed Mr. Fowler and his wife and called upon God in the courtroom to "render unto them double!"

A few months later Sojourner Truth learned that Mr. Fowler, the Alabaman plantation owner, had gone berserk and had brutally murdered his wife, Eliza, the daughter of the same Mrs. Gedney who'd earlier mocked Sojourner's anguish over the loss of her little son. And remembering that she'd asked God to render unto her enemies double, she cried, "Oh, my God! That's too much—I did not mean so much, God!"

Sometimes when we think God does not see our despair, we can remember Sojourner Truth and know that he does—and maybe we can even feel grateful he doesn't always lash out in his rage just to prove we are not without help.

MARY

. . . For your Father knows what you need before you ask him.
—Matthew 6:8b (NIV)

Mary Prince was a West Indies slave in the first half of the nineteenth century. Baptism in August 1817 by Rev. Curtin of the English church was the extent of Mary's Christian teaching. Orphaned by sale at the age of twelve, she was shipped off to begin what turned out to be a life of loneliness and brutal abuse, passed as chattel from one despot to the next. Her autobiography leaves the reader weak with horror. At some point Mr. Wood, one of her "kinder" masters, purchased her for three hundred dollars.

She soon fell so ill with rheumatism she was forced to hobble about with a stick. Then she came down with "Saint Anthony's fire" in her left leg. "No one cared much to come near me," she writes, "and I was ill for a long, long time; for several months I could not lift the limb. I had to lie in a little old outhouse, that was swarming with bugs and other vermin, which tormented me greatly; but I had no other place to lie in. . . . The person who lived in the next yard, (a Mrs. Greene) could not bear to hear my cries and groans. She was kind, and used to send an old slave woman to help me, who sometimes brought me a little soap. When the doctor found I was so ill, he said I must be put into a bath of hot water. The old slave got the bark of some bush that was good for the pains, which she boiled in the hot water, and every night she came and put me into the bath, and did what she could for me; I don't know what I should have done, or what would have become of me, had it not been for her. . . . My mistress did not care to take any trouble about me; and if the Lord had not put it into the hearts of the neighbors to be kind to me, I must, I really think, have lain and died."[10]

But at that time Mary Prince didn't know to ask God to put it into the hearts of the neighbors to be kind. She didn't even know who God was. And yet God answered the prayers she could not speak.

One day Mary Prince was asked to go to a Methodist prayer meeting at the Winthrop's plantation. "I went," she writes, "and they were the first prayers I ever understood." Henry, the husband of the woman who took her, confessed his sins and prayed that God would forgive him. "I felt sorry for my sins also. I cried the whole night, but I was too much ashamed to speak. I prayed God to forgive me. This meeting had a great impression upon my mind, and led my spirit to the Moravian church; so that when I got back to town, I went and prayed to have my name down in the Missionaries' book; and I followed the church earnestly every opportunity."

In time Mr. and Mrs. Wood took a trip to England, and once again God intervened without Mary knowing to ask. After being ordered for the fourth time into the streets alone (to bring her to her senses, claimed the Woods), she found the Moravian church. The church took her in, gave her a place to stay, nursed her tenderly back to health, gave her a means of earning a living, and took her case all the way to Parliament.

After a lifetime of horror and crippling abuse, Mary Prince, without knowing even to ask, was set free. "Thus," she concludes, "I had great cause to bless God in my affliction."

Sometimes we don't have to ask. God already answers, for none of us are ever without help.

CHARLOTTE

In the beginning was the Word, and the Word was with God, and the Word was God. He was with God in the beginning.
—John 1:1 (NIV)

"I have come that they may have life, and have it to the full."
—John 10:10 (NIV)

"You know why they're fattening you up, don't you?

"No," said Wilbur.

"Well, I don't like to spread bad news," said the sheep, "but they're fattening you up because they're going to kill you, that's why."[11]

Do you remember the story *Charlotte's Web?* And how "they," Lurvey, Zuckerman, even John Arable, were going to "murder" poor Wilbur and turn him into smoked bacon and ham? Do you remember, too, what poor Wilbur did? He screamed.

"Stop! . . . I don't want to die! Save me, somebody! Save me! . . . I don't want to die . . . I want to stay alive, right here in my comfortable manure pile with all my friends."

There comes a time in all of our barnyard lives when we realize we're going to die. And oh, how suddenly the manure pile of our lives becomes precious and we squeal in fright as we run in frenzied circles of panic. Oh, please, please, someone save us!

But who *is* going to save us?

In *Charlotte's Web,* Charlotte, the glossy spider of the barnyard, saved Wilbur. By writing words in her web. SOME PIG. TERRIFIC. And finally, at the fair, HUMBLE. And the people were so impressed by this "miracle" pig, Wilbur was set apart as something special, undeserving of his fate, and was thereby saved from being butchered.

In our world, salvation comes to us in a similar fashion—only more spectacularly. The Word came to us in flesh. *In the beginning was the Word, and the Word was with God, and the Word was God.* SOME PIG, TERRIFIC, and finally, HUMBLE. These, and other words, are they not written over our beckoning tombstones? And does not God, reading of our "innocence" and "justification," pass over us, saving us from our fate—as did Charlotte's Words save Wilbur from his? Are we not a "miracle" people—as was Wilbur a "miracle" pig—redeemed by the blood of the Word itself?

Even in the face of death there is hope of a hero. Wilbur had Charlotte. We have the Word. And because of this, even when looking at death we know we are never without help.

HANNAH

There was a certain man from Ramathaim, a Zuphite from the
hill country of Ephraim, whose name was Elkanah .... He had
two wives; one was called Hannah and the other Peninnah.
Peninnah had children, but Hannah had none.

  Year after year this man went up from his town to worship
... at Shiloh.... Whenever the day came for Elkanah to
sacrifice, he would give portions of the meat to his wife
Peninnah and to all her sons and daughters. But to Hannah he
gave a double portion because he loved her, and the Lord had
closed her womb. And because the Lord had closed her womb,
her rival kept provoking her in order to irritate her. This went
on year after year. Whenever Hannah went up to the house of
the Lord, her rival provoked her till she wept and would not
eat. Elkanah her husband would say to her, "Hannah, why are
you weeping? Why don't you eat? Why are you downhearted?
Don't I mean more to you than ten sons?"

  —1 Samuel 1:1–10 (NIV)

The yearly journey to Shiloh was a trying one for Hannah. Though
she was her husband's favorite wife, she had no child, and this was
the most dreaded fear of every woman in a culture where sons
determined a woman's worth. Furthermore, to be without a male
child virtually guaranteed a woman a pauper's widowhood; to be
without *any* child was guaranteed a curse of God. And so to Hannah, journeying year after year to Shiloh, her unanswered prayers
year after year must have stood a mockery more despairing than
the cruel taunts of the unloved wife, Peninnah, with her whole
passel of offspring.

  One year her emotional anguish was so great Hannah wept and
could not eat. "Why are you weeping?" her husband (I think fool-
ishly, but probably more helplessly) asked. "Am I not better to you
than ten sons?"

  Not really. Elkanah was an old man and unable to provide any
economic security for Hannah in a culture in which she would be
reduced quickly to beggary after his death.

The Bible doesn't tell us what she said. It only tells us what she did. She rose and went into the tabernacle to pray.

Hannah was the third woman in biblical history to grieve so bitterly over her inability to conceive. We can only begin to appreciate the seriousness of the problem and the depth of such foreign pain when we see Sarah *giving* her handmaid to her husband and when we see Rachel, loved and cherished by Jacob, crying out in torment, "Give me children, or else I die!" Very few of us have known desperation so deep we would invite another woman to share our husband's bed or feel as though we would surely die. Yet this was the very real pain of Hannah.

"O Lord of hosts," she prayed, spread out before the altar of God, "if thou wilt look on the affliction of thine handmaid, and remember me, and not forget thine handmaid, but wilt give unto thine handmaid a man child, then I will give him unto the Lord all the days of his life." Unlike Sarah and Rachel, Hannah accepted the role of Orphan—and asked for help.

It comes as no surprise, then, to read two verses down, that in time Hannah conceived and bore a son and that she called his name Samuel. "I have asked him of the Lord," she said, and because of Samuel, Hannah learned, Israel learned, and even we learn that we are never without help.

ELIZA

He reached down from on high and took hold of me;
  he drew me out of deep waters.
He rescued me from my powerful enemy,
  from my foes, who were too strong for me.
They confronted me in the day of my disaster,
  but the Lord was my support.
He brought me out into a spacious place;
  he rescued me because he delighted in me.

—Psalm 18:16–19 (NIV)

The most traveled route in the Underground Railroad was that of the Ohio-Kentucky line,[12] where fugitives spilled across the Ohio River into freedom. When Mr. Shelby in *Uncle Tom's Cabin* sold Tom to pay off a debt, he also sold off Eliza's little boy Harry, making one more fugitive to cross the river.

Eliza was a mulatto woman, her four-year-old son a quadroon with silky black curls, a winsome way, and a knack for dance, mime, and song; and who unfortunately had attracted the attention of Mr. Haley, the slave trader. That night, secreted in a closet, Eliza overheard the dreadful news as it was passed from Mr. Shelby to Mrs. Shelby. With trembling hands, Eliza packed a few things into a handkerchief, tied it to her waist, wrote a note to her mistress, gently woke her son, then glided away into the dark of night, her only hope "in God."

She got as far as the Ohio River. "It was early spring," Harriet Beecher Stowe writes, "and the river was swollen and turbulent; great cakes of floating ice were swinging heavily to and fro in the turbid waters. . . . The narrow channel which swept round the bend was full of ice, piled one cake over another . . ." It didn't take Eliza long to see that no ferries were running, but a man, the innkeeper reported, would be taking "some truck this evening, if he durs' to; he'll be in here to supper to-night, so you'd better set down and wait."

Eliza couldn't "set down." She put Harry to sleep but she herself guarded the window. Forty-five minutes later Mr. Haley rode by and Eliza, with Harry quickly plucked from his slumber, was out the back door before Haley could even reach the front, and he caught sight of her just as she disappeared down the bank.

"In that dizzy moment her feet to her," Stowe writes, "scarce seemed to touch the ground, and a moment brought her to the water's edge. Right on behind they came; and, nerved with strength such as God gives only to the desperate, with one wild cry and flying leap, she vaulted sheer over the turbid current by the shore, on to the raft of ice beyond. It was a desperate leap— impossible to anything but madness and despair . . .

"The huge green fragment of ice on which she alighted pitched and creaked as her weight came on it, but she staid there not a moment. With wild cries and desperate energy she leaped to another and still another cake; stumbling—slipping—springing up-wards again! Her shoes were gone—her stockings cut from her feet—while blood marked every step; but she saw nothing, felt nothing, till dimly, as in a dream, she saw the Ohio side, and a man helping her up the bank."

It was Eliza's trust in God, her love for her son, and her own grit that gave her the needed courage to vault a river full of spring ice. And lest anyone think Eliza only a figment of Harriet Beecher Stowe's imagination, a mere twist in a storybook plot, Harriet Beecher Stowe tells us otherwise. The mulatto who crossed the Ohio with her son in the throes of a spring thaw was, back then, a well-known fact. Harriet Beecher Stowe merely gave an unknown woman a name, reminding us again we are never without help.[13]

LISSA

"So I say to you: Ask and it will be given to you; seek and you will find; knock and the door will be opened to you. For everyone who asks receives; he who seeks finds; and to him who knocks, the door will be opened."

—Luke 11:9, 10 (NIV)

When a friend introduced me to Lissa Halls Johnson, author of *Just Like Ice Cream,* she said, "You two are going to like each other. You're both cut from the same cloth."

Lissa and I agree.

We're both short. We're both thin. We're both single. We both have three children and lousy health and worked as legal secretaries after our divorces. We both write books. And we both have had absolute *nightmares* with our cars.

I don't know what it is about single parenting and car troubles, but the two go together. I had a van, a camper van. It started misbehaving the very day I got it and never let up. I never knew when I got in if I'd have to call AAA to give me a jump start. Once I took it to California and was towed three times before I ever got there and spent over six hundred dollars on a new starter, new wiring after an electrical fire, and a new clutch. I've been stranded on godforsaken mountain roads and busy intersections. Clipping sixty down the freeway one day the engine blew. Parts and pieces richocheted everywhere. Of course, I had no money to buy a new car (I was too busy spending money on the old one), and I could hardly afford a brand new twelve-hundred-dollar engine plus the eight-hundred-dollar labor fee for this cute cracker box of nothing but trouble. My only recourse was to rebuild the engine myself— me, a woman who'd once put antifreeze in the oil hole of her Oldsmobile only to discover the oil hole was really the antifreeze hole—the only time in my life utter ignorance ever paid off. Anyway, three months after rebuilding my engine, dual carburetors and all, some nineteen-year-old kid without insurance plowed right into the back end of me, threw the van into a pickup, rolled it upside down in a ditch, and totaled it—and me just about.

My mechanic found me another car. It was worse. It wasn't even cute enough to make up for its sins. A year later I sold it for half of what I paid for it and counted myself blessed. My mechanic, feeling guilty for taking money from the poor, sold me his own car and (knock on wood, cross your fingers, and say your prayers), it's been holding up pretty well. A new radiator now and then and a sticky choke. But hey, who's complaining? It starts up when I climb in.

So it was no surprise when I got a phone call from Lissa not long after her divorce. A car that had once been minding its Ps and Qs just fine had decided to be obnoxious. "Don't tell me," I said. "Universal joint is shot? Pistons eating head gaskets for lunch? Leaky radiator? Broken water pump? Oil taking up shooting practice? Tires need balancing? Rotating? Gone bald? Blow out?"

"You're getting warm."

"Lug nuts snapped and you lost your wheels?"

"Broken axle."

It was all downhill from there. To make a long story short, her father finally had had enough and loaned her the money to buy a used car. But like my Duster, it was a cure worse than the disease. She was *pouring* money into that thing.

"So where's God?" Lissa asked one night when all she could afford for brake shoes were beer cans. "We *could* be giving all this money to the poor, you know."

She called me up another day, and I sat down quickly. Someone had sent her in the mail and—yes, folks, it's one of those money-in-the-mail stories—ten thousand dollars to go buy herself a brand new car.

So for me God provided patience, a lean belt (and a fan belt or two or three), and finally and about time a car that (knock on wood, cross your fingers, and say your prayers) gets me where I need to go. Lissa? Some people are just lucky, I guess.

So Lissa brags about her check in the mail and I brag about rebuilding my Volkswagen engine, and while it may look like she's got the better deal, I do get more mileage out of my story. People are bored with money-in-the-mail stories; they're a dime a dozen. Mine's more interesting. But it does go to show, though, while some of us may get oranges and others of us lemons, none of us, however, are ever without help.

BATHSHEBA

One evening David got up from his bed and walked around on the roof of the palace. From the roof he saw a woman bathing. The woman was very beautiful, and David sent someone to find out about her. The man said, "Isn't this Bathsheba, the daughter of Eliam and the wife of Uriah the Hittite?" Then David sent messengers to get her. She came to him, and he slept with her. . . . Then she went back home. The woman conceived and sent word to David, saying, "I am pregnant."

—2 Samuel 11:2–5 (NIV)

The night was hot when Bathsheba went up to bathe on the top of her home in Jerusalem. She didn't know King David's new palace on the eastern ridge afforded a view of her rooftop, nor that he, unable to sleep that night, had gone up to his own roof to get some air. She only knew that a message arrived the next day—the king summoning her to his palace.

I try to imagine her thoughts as she dressed for the strange, unexplained honor. Or how her thoughts must have turned when

King David informed her she was to comply with his lust. It had to have been a difficult time, a betrayal of trust and honor. And what were her thoughts when she found she was pregnant? By the king? Her husband out of town, serving in the king's army?

The law was clear. Adulterers were to be stoned. And Bathsheba, like so many of us, found herself stuck "between a rock and a hard place" through no fault of her own. What was she to do? Like most Orphans, her first choice to seek help was not specific. She simply sent a note, "*I am pregnant.*" It was up to David to figure it out. She was helpless; he was the king.

For most of us, this is all we can do when first knocked off our feet by tragedy and crisis, and that's okay. When we get back on our feet, we'll learn to be more specific. Which is exactly what happened with Bathsheba.

Years later we see her as only one of eight wives. But we also see her as a woman who'd learned how to be an Orphan; learning her own strength and, in the absence of power, to trust. A difficult task, considering where she started.

King David was old and dying. Adonijah, a son by another wife, was plotting to take over. If he succeeded (and it looked like he would, for he had the endorsement of Joab, the king's military captain), this would put Bathsheba's life in danger—again. And so she went into the king's bedchamber, this time with a *specific* request—and trust in the man David had become.

"My lord," she began, bowing before him, "you swore by the Lord God unto me, your wife, that assuredly Solomon our son would reign and that he would sit upon the throne."[14]

Did David nod, head against the pillow?

"But Adonijah reigns. And you, my lord the king, don't know of this. Even now he has slain oxen and cattle and sheep and has called all the sons of the king, Abiathar the priest, Joab the captain of the host, but he has not called Solomon."

At this point David must have raised up on an elbow and called for more pillows. Solomon's life, Bathsheba's . . .

"You are king," she said, pressing her point, "and all the eyes of Israel are upon you, waiting to see what you will do. Who *shall* sit upon the throne? If you say nothing and Adonijah comes to reign, when my lord is laid to rest with his fathers, then I and my son Solomon will be counted as offenders and perish."

"Bathsheba." I can imagine he held out his hand, remembering again all he'd put her through. "Bathsheba . . . " And slowly she bowed over his hand, confident in her trust.

No longer the helpless Orphan, *take care of me,* Bathsheba had moved into self-reliance, *do this for me.* And David did. "Even as I swore unto you," he said, repentant of past wrong, "by the Lord God who has redeemed my soul from all my distress, assuredly Solomon your son shall reign after me and he shall sit upon the throne in my stead. This day I will see it done."

All the world has benefitted by Bathsheba's strength, given to her in a time of helplessness, for Solomon became the wisest king to ever rule. Today we still read his songs to find beauty, comfort, and wisdom and to be reminded all over again that none of us are ever without help.

CHOOSING

THE ORPHAN ROLE
Discovering Self-Reliance

On the third day Esther put on her royal robes and stood in the inner court of the palace, in front of the king's hall. The king was sitting on his royal throne in the hall, facing the entrance. When he saw Queen Esther standing in the court, he was pleased with her and held out to her the gold scepter that was in his hand. So Esther approached and touched the tip of the scepter.

Then the king asked, "What is it, Queen Esther? What is your request? Even up to half the kingdom, it will be given you."

"If it please the king," replied Esther, "let the king, together with Haman, come today to a banquet I have prepared for him."

"Bring Haman at once," the king said, "so that we may do as Esther asks."

So the king and Haman went to the banquet Esther had prepared. As they were drinking wine, the king again asked Esther, "Now what is your petition?"

—Esther 5:1–6a (NIV)

"**J**ust follow the yellow brick road. Fol . . . low . . . the . . . yel . . . low . . . br–" Dorothy, the Orphan, no sooner gets started on the yellow brick road than she comes to an intersection. She looks around. Which way to the Emerald City, and home? Cornfields stretch as far as eye can see. No good witch, no hero on the horizon. Now what? Which way is she supposed to go?

"Pardon me, that way is a very nice way."

"Who said that?" She turns all around.

"It's pleasant down that way too."

"That's funny," she says, holding fast to Toto and noticing for the first time a Scarecrow dangling from a pole near the intersection. "Wasn't he pointing the other way?"

"Of course, people do go both ways," and the Scarecrow crosses both his arms, fingers pointing in opposite directions.

There is always help. We are never abandoned. There is, however, an element of choice. The Scarecrow did not *tell* Dorothy which way to go. He listed her options, then let her decide. The Orphan's role is not so much about helplessness as it is about choice, of trusting God *and ourselves* so that we may set our teeth to confront the dragons we encounter.

It's a little hard, though, to make choices and to trust when you feel more like Piglet in *Winnie-the-Pooh*. Piglet is an Orphan, dependent upon Christopher Robin for safety and help. Yet Piglet is a very brave little piglet; he has absolute trust in his pals. It's this trust that enables him to do things he normally thinks quite beyond him.

One day Kanga appears in the forest with little Roo in her pocket and the crew declares it best that she go back whence she came. They do not like Kanga. Rather, they are afraid of her: of *anyone* who "pockets" their children. And so Rabbit comes up with a plot. They will hide Roo from Kanga, then only let Kanga know where he is—*if* she will promise to leave the forest, never to return.

Piglet, of course, is afraid to tangle with Kanga, for Kangas are dangerous and he is so very small. But Rabbit says it's *because* he is so very small he will be so helpful.

Piglet, like all good Orphans, immediately forgets his fright in the face of being helpful, for this is what spurs the Orphan on, helping someone else. "Orphans learn," says Carol Pearson, "that there can be some safety and love in the world after they learn to give and to care for others."[15]

And is this not what our fairy tales teach us? Hansel sprinkles breadcrumbs—to save Gretel. Gretel tricks the wicked witch—to save Hansel. Jack climbs the beanstalk—to save his mother from starvation. And even Dorothy, after "proper introductions" to the

Scarecrow, forgets all about herself in concern for him. He is stuck with a pole up his back, and she tries to get him down.

"But—Oh dear, I don't quite see how I can . . . " It's so easy to feel the Orphan again. It's one thing to trust and even want to be helpful, but . . . we can't get the Scarecrow down. Helpless, overwhelmed, the task seems too big after all.

But there is, remember, always help. "Of course I'm not bright about doing things," says the Scarecrow, "but if you'll just bend the nail down in the back, maybe I'll *slip* off and come—oh, yes!" and down he tumbles.

The same goes for Piglet when he finally hears how he is to be helpful. And who can blame him? The task seems a bit big, and very risky. Rabbit has decided Pooh will distract Kanga. Rabbit will then snatch Roo and run. And Piglet? *Just the very size of Roo,* he will pop inside Kanga's pocket! All of a sudden Piglet forgets all about being helpful! He is an Orphan again, helpless, overwhelmed, noble intentions paling in light of his fear! Because what will happen when Kanga discovers Piglet is not Roo?

But the Scarecrow helped Dorothy. "If you'll just bend the nail down a bit—" And so Rabbit helps Piglet. He's not in it alone; his buddies will be right there with him. And so off they all go, Piglet, Pooh, and Rabbit, to look for Kanga.

All very well, I suppose, for children's stories and fairy tales. But what of real Orphans? Trust and being helpful only get us so far. Dragons and crises are not so easily humored. Our own helplessness is not always so easily overcome. How do we confront dragons and get away with it, *fait accompli?*

Barbara Carlson, former counseling coordinator of the Womencare Shelter in Bellingham, Washington, says that a battered woman will attempt a break from her abuse an average of seven times before making a final break. When crisis first interrupts our lives and dumps us outside of Eden we're often so traumatized all we can do is whimper, and it's a difficult task to sort out what we *can* do from what it feels we *can't.* Only time can foster the self-confidence needed to make the necessary choices whenever we run up against the dragons. It helps, I think, to approach the dragon in little steps, proceeding *very carefully.*

In the Bible we can see what Queen Esther did in 883 B.C.

The Jews were to be slaughtered on the thirteenth day of the twelfth month in the twelfth year of King Xerxes' reign by order of Haman, the king's right-hand man. And Queen Esther, the king's queen, was the only one who could plead the cause of her people. It was risky, yes; she had been in disfavor for some thirty days. Yet when the king held out his golden scepter she did not immediately fall to her knees and beg for mercy. She approached this dragon one step at a time, *asking only for what she felt capable of obtaining.*

"If it please the king," she said, drawing herself up tall and smiling well, "let the king and Haman come this day to a dinner I have prepared for the king." She held little power or confidence, but this she could do, she could ask the king to dinner.

That night the king asked, "What is your petition?" curious now that his stomach was full. "It shall be granted you. And what is your request? Even to the half of my kingdom, it shall be fulfilled."

Esther held back. She was a beautiful woman; the king, she saw, was intrigued. *But did she have the confidence to make her request?* "If I have found favor in the sight of the king," she said, "and if it please the king to grant my petition and fulfill my request, let the king and Haman come tomorrow to the dinner which I will prepare for them, and tomorrow I will do as the king has said."

The next night she prayerfully applied her toilet, and again served her dinner.

"What is your petition, Queen Esther?" said the king, reclining with a glass of wine and a smile upon his face. "It shall be granted to you. And what is your request? Even to the half of my kingdom, it shall be fulfilled."

They spoke with their eyes. "Tell me," the husband said. "Dare I?" said the wife. Haman shifted. The mood in the room had swung in the exchange.

"Let my life be given me at my petition," said Esther, then waited for the effect in her husband's eyes and when she got what she wanted, added, "and my people at my request."

There was a flurry of spilled wine. Haman turned white.

"We are sold, I and my people, to be destroyed, to be slain, and to be slaughtered." A pin could be heard if dropped. She told everything Haman had schemed. "If we had been sold merely as slaves," she whispered, "I would have held my peace. Our affliction would not be compared with the loss to the king." She did not take her eyes from the king's.

This is the way an Orphan resolves conflict. Because we know there is a hero, we can accept our powerlessness and not be over-whelmed by it; there is someone to turn to. We needn't panic, whine, or manipulate our environment and everyone in it in the hopes that someone will take pity on us and come rushing in to save the day. Instead we *trust* in God. We make choices based on *helping* others. And then we proceed, one *risky* step at a time—discovering our own power along the way as others respond and validate who we are. We then *ask* for help from a position of *our* power, not *circumstantial* powerlessness. Trust, help, risk, ask. Haman was hung, and the Jews were spared.

Last week, about five o'clock on a Friday night, my sons hol-lered that the basement was full of water. I turned off the com-puter and took a peek. Water all right. Two inches of it. Everywhere.

My immediate reaction was that of helpless Orphan. Holy shmoly, I thought, absolutely overwhelmed. *What was I going to do?* Washer and dryer sat in a lake, along with the laundry basket, the boys' dresser, their beds, toy boxes, bikes, scooters, car tires, old boxes and Christmas decorations, suitcases, lawn mower, last summer's fan, and an old stereo and speakers. Baseball cards floated by. I couldn't think. I was Dorothy standing in the middle of the intersection. Then slowly my choices came to me, as if some Scarecrow in my mind was pointing them all out.

"You can call your landlord," said the Scarecrow, pointing his arm one direction. "Or you can call the fire department," pointing the other way. "Or," he said, crossing his arms, "you can try han-dling it yourself."

What? Just me and a tin can? Are you crazy? I chose not to handle it myself. Orphans don't always have to decide to go it alone. Besides, it was the landlord's responsibility. But how were they going to get rid of the water? I picked up the phone, and even as I was punching 911 I was pulling on my boots. An Orphan so long, the process was playing itself out unconsciously in my mind. Trust, help, risk, ask. "Do you ever," I asked the fireman, "pump water out of people's basements?"

Then I called the landlord. "I got the fire department," I told him, pleased I could offer more than just a panicked "HELP!" on a Friday night, "coming over to pump the basement. But you and

Bruce probably ought to take a look at this, or I'll be needing a rowboat to do my laundry and kiss my boys goodnight."

They all arrived in due time, three firemen in galoshes and helmets, Frank and Bruce with a sump pump. One look around, though, and I could see there was nothing else I could do but get in the way. "Hey, I can't stand it," I told them all, water sloshing around my ankles. "I'll be over at my neighbor's if you need me, okay?" And over I went and had a nice cup of tea, glorying in my power as an Orphan. I'd never felt better about being so helpless.

When up against the dragon, the Orphan becomes a role we *choose*, not one we fall into.

So which way did Dorothy choose to go? Rewind the video. "Won't you take me with you?" the Scarecrow asks. He wants to go see the Wizard; he wants the Wizard to give him a brain.

Dorothy agrees and off they go. "We're off to see the Wizard," they sing, but off in which direction?

Rewind the video again. Surprisingly, in *neither* of the directions pointed out by the Scarecrow. Dorothy, her initial Orphan panic subdued by the help of the Scarecrow, discovers in being helpful her own ability to accomplish. This surge of self-reliance sees her on her *own* way—straight ahead. She is no longer choosing the role of Orphan, but that of Pilgrim—she is thinking for herself instead of asking for help. And we're ready for another phase of the inner journey down the yellow brick road toward the hero and redemption we seek. We are ready to begin thinking for ourselves.

NOTES

1. Esther 4:11 (RSV).

2. Personal conversation.

3. M. Scott Peck, *The Road Less Traveled* (New York: Simon & Schuster, 1978), 16.

4. Carol Pearson, *The Hero Within* (San Francisco: Harper & Row, 1986), 33.

5. J. E. Cirlot, *A Dictionary of Symbols* (New York: Philosophical Library, 1962), 296.

6. Peck, *The Road Less Traveled,* 43.

7. Esther 4:16 (paraphrased) (RSV).

8. Romans 10:17 (RSV).

9. Virginia Ortiz, *Sojourner Truth: A Self Made Woman* (Philadelphia: Lippincott, 1974).

10. Mary Prince, "The History of Mary Prince" in Henry Louis Gates, Jr., ed., *The Classic Slave Narrations* (New York: New American Library, 1987), 187–215.

11. E. B. White, *Charlotte's Web* (New York: Harper & Row), 1952, 49–51.

12. Charles L. Blockson, *The Underground Railroad* (New York: Berkeley, 1989), 73.

13. Harriet Beecher Stowe, *Uncle Tom's Cabin, or Life Among The Lowly* (Boston: John P. Jewett, 1852), 107–108, 117–118, 618.

14. 1 Kings 1:17 (paraphrased) (RSV).

15. Pearson, *The Hero Within,* 37.

FOUR *P*ILGRIM

"I am going to run from this dragon!"

—*Hagar the Pilgrim*

THINKING FOR OURSELVES
Fleeing Expectation to Quest Identity

Then Sarai dealt harshly with her, and she fled from her. The angel of the Lord found her by a spring of water in the wilderness, the spring on the way to Shur. And he said, "Hagar, maid of Sarai, where have you come from and where are you going?" She said, "I am fleeing from my mistress Sarai."

... So she called the name of the Lord who spoke to her, "Thou are a God of seeing"; for she said, "Have I really seen God and remained alive after seeing him?"

—Genesis 16:6–8, 13 (RSV)

If the Orphan confronts the dragon by seeking rescue—and learning self-reliance; the Pilgrim confronts the dragon by escape—and learning to think for oneself. "How do you do?" Dorothy had asked the Scarecrow politely at the intersection of the yellow brick road.

"Oh, I'm not feeling at *all* well," the Scarecrow responds honestly. "You see, it's very tedious being stuck up here all day long with a pole up your back." The Scarecrow is ready to admit his captivity, and that he yearns to escape.

Ironically, the Scarecrow is being held captive in a garden where everything should be just fine. Yet it isn't. His job is to scare away crows but there they are, sitting on his shoulder and cawing in his ear. He can't figure it out, and the longer he hangs there, the more ineffective he becomes, until finally he begins to chafe at the contradictions of his life and is ready to admit *things are not the way they are supposed to be.*

A lot of us are like this. We're doing what we should, yet nothing is getting done. We're just hanging out, dangling from poles erected for us by our culture, our church, our parents, friends, husbands, children, bosses. Who are *we*? Stuffed with everyone else's expectations, we don't know anymore. We may never have known. "But this," we're told, "is as good as it gets." So we settle in, and our garden becomes our cage.

We can spend a lot of time being a Scarecrow, pole up our back and not feeling at all well, listening to the voices all around that tell us to stay put, do our job, make no waves, just "hang in there." Ears open, we listen; eyes shut, we blind ourselves to the crows flying in from miles around just to eat in our field and laugh in our face. Dutifully we hang, living in alienation with ourselves—and, like the Scarecrow, ineffective in the world around us.

We get this way because somewhere along the line we've chosen not to think for ourselves. But crisis strikes and wakes us up. Scarecrows do not scare crows. *Caw, caw!* Crows and contradiction fly in our faces. Wives, do not leave your husbands. *But he's beating me to death!* Pray for one another that you may be healed. *But my baby died!* Bring up a child in the way that he should go, and when he is old he shall not depart from it. *But Fred ran away from home!* When he is old—*You don't understand! He died! Thirteen years old! Caw!* What is really happening here? we have to ask ourselves. What are we doing? What do we believe? Crows and contradiction clamor, and if ever we're going to resolve our conflict, we have to start thinking for ourselves again. We cannot afford to let the dragons win while we rot in confusion, and down we tumble from our poles, stumbling and tripping, getting back up and falling back down, wobbly on our feet—with a decision to make.

Are we going to stay put, living in contradiction, our lives defined by someone else? Or are we going to start thinking again and flee such captivity?

"Brenda, when you get finished with those transcriptions I want you to call the court reporter and set up a time for that deposition next week. Then call the courthouse to find out what calendar I'm on for the Smith case, and do only side two of the tape, and be sure to make three copies, one for . . . "

I remember staring at the stack of legal files beside my IBM Selectric, hearing my attorney boss's voice going on and on, and thinking bleakly, almost helplessly, *What am I doing here?*

"Oh, and Brenda!" he hollered from his window-walled office across the hall from my small cubicle. "When Mr. Kelly comes in, two coffees!"

I was a writer, not a legal secretary, but I had allowed the divorce courts to assign me a role that contradicted who I was. I was told to get a "real" job, and so, like the Scarecrow, I was living out someone else's expectations, miserably unhappy and at war with myself. Exhausted, in and out of the hospital with stress-exasperated illnesses, and with my three-year-old son spending his day-care hours huddled beneath a table behind a wall of silence, I felt trapped, pole up my back, by what someone had told me was the responsible thing to do. And because I'd quit thinking for myself, the dragons were winning.

The Pilgrim is one who dares to think and, if need be, flee. When conflict reaches a point where it no longer provides room for personal growth or the development of who God created us to be, the Pilgrim chooses to retreat and redirect. In *Pilgrim's Progress* Christian fled the City of Destruction for "Life! life! everlasting life!" Odysseus, in the *Odyssey,* fled the nymph Calypsos for Penelope. We flee jobs that don't satisfy, relationships that solidify into abuse, and ideologies that no longer hold up.

"There is no problem too big, too horrendous, too overwhelming, or too impossible—that you can't run away from." So says my friend Laura Kalpakian. And she's right. Peter Rabbit ran for his life, as well he should have. What else is there to do when Mr. McGregor is plowing through onions and radishes after us brandishing a hoe? This is not the time for "working it through." Sometimes we forget, that when up against the dragon, we *can* run.

It's not an easy choice, though. Flight is not readily endorsed by our culture. The Martyr looks upon it as selfish, the Warrior as weak. The Orphan sees it as dangerous. Even we feel guilty for abandoning our conflict. It smacks of irresponsibility. Yet the role of Pilgrim is not so much a choice for flight and escape *as it is a choice for quest.* "Do you think if I went with you," the Scarecrow sighs, "this Wizard would give me some brains?" It's abandoning who we've been told we are so we can explore who we really are. It's setting aside what other people think in order to discover what we really believe. As Tim Hansel talks about in *You Gotta Keep Dancin',* it's turning our theology into biography[1]—and there's nothing like contradictions in our lives to propel us on our way.

John Calvin writes at the beginning of his *Institutes:* "Our wisdom . . . consists almost entirely of two parts: the knowledge of God and ourselves."[2] God we know, but ourselves? Most of us have no idea. We are not without help, however.

There is an inner voice in all of us (independent of heads stuffed full of straw!) that begins to whisper whenever we live in contradiction with who we are. "Brenda," the inner voice whispered each time I slid another piece of paper into the carriage, "you can do so much more with yourself than just typing interrogatories. You can write *books!*"

Having never published one, I was unsure; it seemed a bit lofty. All around me friends and foe alike argued. "Pipe dream," they all agreed, and I banged out THE SUPERIOR COURT OF THE COUNTY OF KING.

Bruce Larson in *Ask Me to Dance* wrote in rebuttal, however. "Our hunger," he wrote, "to be bigger than we are could be just delusions of grandeur or it could be the very voice of God inside calling us to a larger inheritance, to a bigger stake in reality, to a truer sense of our identity as the sons and daughters of God."[3]

But when, the Scarecrow inside of me asked, is dissatisfaction with my life to be interpreted as the "very voice of God," and when is it something that ought to be worked through? When is discontent God's signal for better things or when is it simply the lazy way out?

Tresa Wiggins suggests that whenever we find ourselves up against discontent and contradiction, we try asking, "What person do I think God wants me to be and how best can I be that person?"

It's a good question to ask, for it gets us thinking again. *What person do I think God wants me to be and how best can I be that person?* "What person do *I* (not someone else) think *God* (not someone else) wants *me* (not someone else) to be and how best can *I* (not someone else) be that person?" I couldn't be that person typing interrogatories. The Scarecrow couldn't be that person in a cornfield with a pole up his back. And even naughty old Peter Rabbit couldn't be that person—made into rabbit pie.

The Pilgrim's role, then, is a choice we make to think for ourselves, a choice which requires some form of flight, and quest. It's pulling back from all the *shoulds* of life so we can discover our own goals. It's setting aside other people's opinions, ideas, mandates, and judgments in order to analyze our own. Finally, it's daring to act on our own truth. Perhaps Mr. McGregor is wrong and we don't make good rabbit pie. Perhaps we're not Scarecrows after all, and that's why all the crows are cawing in our ears.

Whenever I get uneasy about the choice of flight in the midst of conflict as a valid option, I open my Bible to Genesis 16 and 21. Hagar, a handmaid of Sarai and pregnant with Abram's child, was a bit like the Scarecrow in *The Wizard of Oz*. She had to flee the role she'd been assigned—for something had gone wrong. Sarai abused her.

At first God sent Hagar back to her mistress, and if we stop here in the story we might well conclude that God endorses and seals the definitions others place upon us. But he did not send her back as handmaid—and this is the difference. He sent her back knowing who she *really* was. She was mother of Ishmael, mother of multitudes, *a woman who had seen God—and lived.*

For a time it seems Sarai and Abram were content to allow Hagar her real identity. But fourteen years later, when Isaac was born to Sarai, the abuse began again. Sarai says it was because Hagar laughed at Isaac, yet did not Isaac's name mean "Laughter"? I think the bigger truth was that Sarai simply could not tolerate the *real* Hagar anymore. The *real* Hagar was a perceived threat (now that Isaac was born), and so she instructed Abram to "cast out this *slave* woman and her son" (emphasis mine).

This time God did not send Hagar back. There was no point. When conflict is so solidified we cannot *be who we are,* it's time to flee for good and embrace that which God calls us to be. "Hagar?" God called. "What troubles you?" He invites us, in the loneliness of our flight, to pour out our fears, our confusion, our anger and rage, our sense of betrayal, our helplessness, our loss of self. And then he says to us, as he did to Hagar, "Fear not, for I have heard."

Hagar opened her eyes and saw water, God's provision for her pilgrimage, her flight and quest. He does the same for us.

Even so, it's a scary, risky time. In *The Wizard of Oz* Dorothy is smart enough to warn the Scarecrow of the danger. "Do you think" he has asked her, "if I went with you this Wizard would give me some brains?"

Dorothy tells him, "Maybe you better not. I've got a witch mad at me and you might get into trouble."

Very clearly, the inner journey of the Pilgrim is a dangerous venture. When we think, we sometimes think differently from the status quo—and few appreciate those who march to the beat of a different drum. We might find ourselves terribly misunderstood and "punished."

The Scarecrow, though, had the determination it takes. "Witch? Humph. I'm not afraid of anything. Oh, dear . . . except a lighted match."

"I don't blame you for that."

"But I'd face a whole boxful of them for the chance of getting some brains."

To think for ourselves requires tremendous courage. We have to face the empty desert like Hagar and the boxful of matches like the Scarecrow. Yet the Pilgrim marches on, courageous enough to face the unknown.

"Won't you take me with you?" the Scarecrow asks again.

And here is an interesting point. Dorothy agrees—because even if the Wizard couldn't give the Scarecrow some brains, he would be no worse off than before.

"Yes," says the Scarecrow, "that's true."

But this is only fairy tale, remember? We, unlike the Scarecrow, do have a guarantee. We have the echo of God's whisper to Hagar, "Do not fear, I have heard." God stands ready with water to ease our thirst, to grant meaning to our lives the minute we dare the Pilgrim's inner journey of flight and quest.

CHRISTIAN

And afterward Moses and Aaron went in, and told Pharaoh, Thus saith the Lord God of Israel, Let my people go, that they may hold a feast unto me in the wilderness.

And Pharaoh said, Who is the Lord, that I should obey his voice to let Israel go? I know not the Lord, neither will I let Israel go.

And they said, The God of the Hebrews hath met with us: let us go, we pray thee, three days' journey into the desert, and sacrifice unto the Lord our God; lest he fall upon us with pestilence, or with the sword.

And the king of Egypt said unto them, Wherefore do ye, Moses and Aaron, let the people from their works? get you unto your burdens. And Pharaoh said, Behold, the people of the land now are many, and ye make them rest from their burdens. And Pharaoh commanded the same day the taskmasters of the people, and their officers, saying, Ye shall no more give the people straw to make brick, as heretofore: Let them go and gather straw for themselves. And the tale of the bricks, which they did make heretofore, ye shall lay upon them; ye shall not diminish ought thereof; for they be idle; therefore they cry, saying, Let us go and sacrifice to our God. Let there be more work laid upon the men, that they may labor therein; and let them not regard vain words.

And the taskmasters of the people went out, and their officers, and they spake to the people, saying, Thus saith Pharaoh, I will not give you straw. Go ye, get you straw where ye can find it; yet not ought of your work shall be diminished.

—Exodus 5:1–11 (KJV)

A man clothed in rags stood with a burden upon his back, book in hand, reading and weeping, "What shall I do?" At home he could not hide his grief and burden, and to his wife and children he cried, "[I am] undone by reason of a burden that lieth hard upon me; moreover, I am certainly informed that this our city will be burned with fire from heaven; in which . . . myself, with thee, my wife, and you, my sweet babes, shall miserably come to ruin, except . . . some way of escape can be found whereby we may be delivered."[4]

Something was wrong in the City of Destruction, and Christian had no idea what it was. All he knew was the burden on his back, heavy after reading of condemnation and judgment.

Evangelist, meeting him in the fields where he paced the earth, asked, "Why not willing to die, since this life is attended with so many evils?"

"Because I fear that this burden that is upon my back will sink me lower than the grave, and I shall fall into hell."

"If this be thy condition, why standest thou still?"

"Because I know not whither to go."

Evangelist unrolled a parchment.

"*Flee from the wrath to come?* But whither must I fly?" asked Christian.

"Do you see yonder shining light? Keep that light in your eye, and go up directly thereto: so that thou see the gate; at which, when thou knockest, it shall be told thee what thou shalt do."

Christian began to run, but his wife and children, seeing him, entreated him to return. He put his fingers in his ears, shutting out their cries, and ran on crying, "Life! life! eternal life!"

The neighbors came out. Some mocked, others threatened, still others begged him to return. Two even pursued to hold him back by force.

Whenever we flee, turning our backs on what we've been taught and are expected to do, we can be guaranteed resistance. People will entreat, mock, and threaten. A few will even get nasty, pursuing and holding us back by force—just as Pliable and Obstinate did with Christian, and as Pharaoh of Egypt did with the Hebrews of so long ago.

But neither Christian nor Moses let anyone stop them. "You dwell," Christian told his friends, "in the City of Destruction. Be content, good neighbors, and go along with me."

"What!" said Obstinate. "And leave our friends and comforts behind us?"

"Yes, because that which you forsake is not worthy to be compared with a little of that I am seeking to enjoy."

"What are the things you seek, since you leave all the world to find them?"

"I seek an inheritance incorruptible, undefiled, and that fadeth not away."

Pliable and Obstinate did not go with him and Christian went on alone, as all Pilgrims must do. Yet in the end he gained what he sought, entrance to the City of Resurrection and understanding, for clarity is always ours when we finally dare the Pilgrim's journey of flight and quest.

RIZPAH

During the war between the house of Saul and the house of David, Abner had been strengthening his own position in the house of Saul. Now Saul had a concubine named Rizpah daughter of Aiah. And Ish-Bosheth said to Abner, "Why did you sleep with my father's concubine?"

Abner was very angry because of what Ish-Bosheth said and he answered, "Am I a dog's head—on Judah's side? This very day I am loyal to the house of your father Saul and to his family and friends. I haven't handed you over to David. Yet now you accuse me of an offense involving this woman! May God deal with Abner, be it ever so severely, if I do not do for David what the Lord promised him on oath and transfer of kingdom from the house of Saul and establish David's throne over Israel and Judah from Dan to Beersheba." Ish-Bosheth did not dare to say another word to Abner, because he was afraid of him.

Then Abner sent messengers on his behalf to say to David, "Whose land is it? Make an agreement with me, and I will help you bring all Israel over to you."

—2 Samuel 3:6–12 (NIV)

Her master beheaded, Rizpah fell heir to Ish-Bosheth, Saul's son and reigning ruler of Israel, but was appropriated by Abner, Saul's general and regent. The two men quarreled over her, and one can't help but wonder about the charm and delight of a woman who would come between a man's general and his son. The quarrel at any rate was of sufficient intensity to split the loyalties in the falling house of Saul. Abner sold out to David, heralding the beginning of the end for the house of Saul.

Within months David held the throne of both Judah and Israel, but all was not well. Famine plagued the land. And at the end of three years, David, to appease Jehovah, had five of Saul's grandchildren hanged, along with the two sons of Saul and Rizpah. Rizpah, once a concubine who wore queenly gowns, donned the garments of sackcloth to mourn her sons—and to grieve the barrenness of a land that had brought about the tragedy.

The seven men were not buried, but left to hang from the gallows to decompose and finally to slip from the nooses to splatter over hot rock below. Rizpah's name has been passed down not only as a woman who knew tragedy, but as a woman who endured stoically in the midst of unparalleled aloneness. For five months she kept watch over her sons' bodies so that no further dishonor could be done and, as some commentators interpret the spreading of her sackcloth over the ground, to honor a pledge with God that she would watch over them until he relented and sent the rains.[5]

Edith Deen writes in *All the Women of the Bible* that through heat of day and chill of night, Rizpah "remained near those sunscorched, weird, blackened, dishonored bodies, watching closely to save them from further harm. Now standing, now sitting, now half dead with sleepiness, and then quivering with daring effort, she drove away the dogs and vultures that would have devoured her dead."[6]

Alone on her weary rock Rizpah kept the vigil as days passed into weeks, weeks into months. Passersby must have paused to watch curiously, some to pity, some perhaps to mock. Others may have even taunted, called her mad. I should think she had to have gone a little mad as she watched the swarms of flies and hornets eat the draining eye sockets of sons she once nursed. But she did not turn back, alone on her Pilgrim's journey.

Sometimes the task of the Pilgrim is brutally lonely, exacting every ounce of stamina and fortitude we can command. Yet, like Rizpah, there is an end; there is quest realized. David heard of Rizpah's vigilance and sent word for the remains to be buried in the family grave at Zelah, along with the bones of Saul and

Jonathan, recovered from Jabesh-gilead, where they'd been interred.

I can imagine Rizpah lurking in the background, sackcloth ragged and filthy with dust, eyes lined, face worn, bowing her head even as the first drops of rain splattered the earth. I see her picking up speed as she pads down the hill to a home she has not entered in five months, lifting the latch to slip inside alone just as the torrential downpour begins, the dreadful famine at long last broken.

The power of flight and quest.

ELIZABETH

Then the King will say to those on his right, "Come, you who are blessed by my Father; take your inheritance, the kingdom prepared for you since the creation of the world. For I was hungry and you gave me something to eat, I was thirsty and you gave me something to drink, I was a stranger and you invited me in, I needed clothes and you clothed me, I was sick and you looked after me, I was in prison and you came to visit me."

Then the righteous will answer him, "Lord, when did we see you hungry and feed you, or thirsty and give you something to drink? When did we see you a stranger and invite you in, or needing clothes and clothe you? When did we see you sick or in prison and go to visit you?"

The King will reply, "I tell you the truth, whatever you did for one of the least of these brothers of mine, you did for me."
—Matthew 25:34–40 (NIV)

No other woman in American history captures the heart of the Pilgrim more fully than Elizabeth Cady Stanton, daughter of a judge, wife of a politician, mother of numerous children, and leader of the women's suffrage movement. From her pen came the immortal words of the Declaration of Sentiments, read at the Seneca Falls Women's Rights Convention, July 1848.

> We hold these truths to be self-evident; that all men and women are
> created equal; that they are endowed by their Creator with certain
> inalienable rights; that among these are life, liberty, and the pursuit of
> happiness . . . [7]

To our ears today there seems to be nothing blasphemous about
this statement, but in 1848 the words fell upon the ears of a pop-
ulace that systematically denied women the right to vote, the right
to own property, the right to their children, the right to keep their
earnings, the right to testify against their husbands in a court of
law, the right to occupations other than teaching, domestics, or
writing, the right to equal pay for equal work, and the right to
higher education. While single women could hold property, they
had to pay taxes without the right to vote, the very issue—taxation
without representation—that, as Lois W. Banner points out in *Women's America,* triggered the Revolutionary War.[8] To Elizabeth,
these and other grievances contradicted the democratic and religious philosophy into which she'd been born, and it took a Pilgrim's journey before she could stand before the nation to
confront the glaring contradiction.

The journey was difficult and lonely, precipitated not so much
by political ideology, however, but by the crying of her first baby.
The standard of the early 1840s called for babies to be wrapped in
swaddling clothes, tight wrappings that restricted movement of
their arms and legs, closed windows to keep out evil substances,
continuous feeding to prevent colic and rickets, and herbal con-
coctions dosed with laudanum. Baby Daniel, however, cried con-
tinuously under this regime and Elizabeth "wept, prayed, and
philosophized by turns."[9] Finally, defying her husband, parents,
doctor, and friends, she threw out the swaddling clothes, opened
the windows, tossed out the medications, fed Danny at regular
intervals—and the results were amazing. The baby stopped crying.

"I learned," said Elizabeth, "a lesson in self-reliance." In short,
she started to think for herself and set a pattern she would never
break.

Today we look at her and applaud, but back then no one
clapped. For eight long years, while birthing and raising numerous
children in quick succession, she immersed herself in the study of
theology, law, and history in order to untangle the prevailing and
illogical notion that women were spiritually and legally inferior to

men. Her spiritual quest took her right to the Quakers, who had no theological difficulties with the equality of women. Together she and Lucretia Mott, a renowned Quaker preacher, organized the first women's rights convention, basing their arguments for equality on Scripture.

It was to be a local affair, for neither of them had solidified in their minds how public they were willing to go with what was fast becoming a controversial issue. When the convention turned into an audience of over three hundred, including forty men, they lost all confidence and corralled Lucretia's husband into chairing the meeting.

The second day, though, brought a change. It was a day devoted to reading Elizabeth's Declaration of Sentiments, and her voice, empowered by the authority of her own hard-searched convictions, electrified the nation.

> The history of mankind is a history of repeated injuries and usurpations on the part of man toward woman, having its direct object the establishment of an absolute tyranny over her. To prove this, let the facts be submitted to a candid world.[10]

The "facts" were picked up by telegraph and for the first time newspapers around the country addressed the topic seriously. The women's suffrage movement was born, and Elizabeth, a housewife who'd dared to think for herself, was propelled into the limelight.

There were to be a lot of ups and downs before her ideas were finally acknowledged by passage of the Nineteenth Amendment, but Elizabeth Cady Stanton had found her footing and stride. Flight from a crying baby's swaddled arms to the quest of political freedom for those who, in 1848, were the "least of brethren," Elizabeth Cady Stanton had at last taken her stand—and she was not going to back down. She had a higher call, as do we all in the face of contradiction—that of flight and quest.

MARY (NOT MARTHA)

As Jesus and his disciples were on their way, he came to a village where a woman named Martha opened her home to him. She had a sister called Mary, who sat the Lord's feet listening to what he said. But Martha was distracted by all the preparations that had to be made. She came to him and asked, "Lord, don't you care that my sister has left me to do all the work by myself? Tell her to help me!"

"Martha, Martha," the Lord answered, "you are worried and upset about many things, but only one thing is needed. Mary has chosen what is better, and it will not be taken away from her."

—Luke 10:38–42 (NIV)

My favorite woman in the Bible has always been Mary of Bethany, for I hate to cook. Actually, the only household chore I enjoy doing is hanging out the laundry. Everything else is a necessary evil. So I was thrilled and joyed-over when my kids got old enough to vacuum, dust, scrub, and wash—for Martha I am not.

Funny, you know Mary is there, but cultural mandate is so strong you can spend years feeling guilty over *not* being Martha. And as "enlightened" as I think I am, I can still feel guilty about the dustballs under the couch and behind the bed, particularly when my mother comes over. And I suppose, if Christ were to drop by, I could get into a dither every bit as bad as poor Martha.

Yet Christ teaches us a better way—Mary's way.

Mary and Martha were sisters of Lazarus, and it appears they all lived in Martha's comfortable home in Bethany, along the Jericho Road. It was a pleasant walk from there to the Mount of Olives and the Temple in Jerusalem, and Jesus, walking back and forth, often stopped over to enjoy his friends' hospitality—and no doubt Martha's cooking.

The night was warm and balmy when Jesus stopped in with his disciples. Mary left the oppressive heat of the kitchen to sit at his feet. He was always so interesting, his ideas thought provoking and even dangerous, for he never hesitated to contradict the religious and political ideologies of just about everyone around. Martha, however, flour and sweat itching around her neck, bread in the oven, wine not chilled quite right, was not amused by this flight from responsibility. She knew better than to confront Mary, though. Mary was always off in a cloud, never doing what she was supposed to. So she spoke to Jesus.

"Jesus," she said, "don't you care that Mary's left me to do all this serving by myself? Tell her to come help me."

"Martha, Martha," he answered, and I can just hear his voice, tender, compassionate, but irritated. "You have gotten yourself in such a flap, and for what? Do we need all these cheese squares and crackers? Look. Look at Mary. She's listening to me, she's thinking." And then comes the line endorsing a Pilgrim's flight and quest. "She has chosen the better way, Martha, *and I won't take that from her.*"

Mary dared to flee the roles of womanhood long enough to quest after Christ, and we see her again at Christ's feet just six days before Passover. The growing threats of the Pharisees had depressed the gathered crowd and she came up softly behind Christ to pour a costly perfume, a pound of ointment of spikenard, over his feet and to wipe his feet with her hair.

It was the custom of the day to bathe and anoint with fragrance a visitor's feet, for the roads were hot and dusty. Martha, knowing the sadness of her master, no doubt joined Mary in an expression of love, perhaps handing him a goblet of cold water drawn fresh from the well. Judas Iscariot, however, interrupted the tenderness.

"Why wasn't this perfume sold," he demanded, grabbing for the precious bottle, "and the money given to the poor? This!" he cried, "is worth a year's wages!"

Jesus must have looked Judas straight in the eye before uttering what has to be a lonely statement. "Leave her alone. Against the day of my burying she has kept this."[11] Did he lay his hand upon Mary's head while Judas, without further word, handed back the precious perfume—worth three times what he would get from the Pharisees for betraying his Lord?

I like to think of Christ in the Garden of Gethsemane a week later, disciples asleep, alone yet comforted by memory of Mary—a woman who dared to take her journey of flight and quest.

BRENDA

A woman who had suffered from severe bleeding for twelve
years came up behind Jesus and touched the edge of his cloak.
She said to herself, "If only I touch his cloak, I will get well."
Jesus turned around and saw her, and said, "Courage, my
daughter! Your faith has made you well." At that very moment
the woman became well.

—Matthew 9:20–22 (TEV)

"I'll be back in half an hour!" I hollered to my three kids, six, eight,
and eleven, as I sprinted out the front door, asthma inhaler in hand.
Eight o'clock, and the May evening was perfect for my two-mile
jog along the lake. A balmy night, a bit of a breeze blowing off the
water.

I was coming back when I felt my lungs tighten. No problem.
I took a whiff of my inhaler and kept running. Another puff. Things
started to ring in my head. What was happening? My tongue, I
noticed, was getting fat. And my nose, my throat. I fought for
breath and slowed to a walk, eyes fogging, heart pounding and
jumping around erratically in my chest now. Pain ripped across my
abdomen, cramps that nearly took me to my knees. I was stumbling now, my breathing labored and tight and getting worse with
each draw. My inhaler was useless. How long had it been since I'd
had a full-blown asthma attack?

But this wasn't asthma. I banged on the door of a stranger's
house. "Call 911," I blurted, then sank to a bench. By now breathing was impossible, and the cramps were so severe I might as well
have been in heavy labor. Pain and lack of oxygen blotted out
everything twelve inches from my face, now so swollen I couldn't
recognize myself by touch. Eyes, nose, lips.

I heard the ambulance wailing down the hill, the commotion of
men gathering round. I could see *nothing* now. I could only hear
frantic voices amidst the wild ringing in my ears.

"Asthma attack!" someone hollered.

"No . . . more than that. The pain . . . " I pointed to my abdomen. "Epinephrine," I gagged, praying they would quit talking and
just get an IV into me. "Cortisone," I whispered, begging.

Someone gave me an injection; I felt the blessed sting. Then the IV, cold in my veins. And I was being hustled, sitting up, into the ambulance.

I've been rushed to the emergency room for asthma attacks so often I know by heart the medications needed and the doses. This was my first concern, to get me breathing again. But I couldn't make the doctor understand the seriousness of what was happening internally. The pain, if possible, was worse. "Maybe it's lack of oxygen," was all he said.

"No, something else is wrong. This is not asthma. I don't swell with asthma. I don't *hurt* like this." When he shrugged again I said, "Call my doctor in Seattle."

He wouldn't do it. He wanted to take a chest X-ray instead and gave the orders.

"No!" I fought the panic of being stuck with an idiot who couldn't see that something far more serious was going on inside my body than a simple asthma attack. I was breathing a little easier, but my body was dying. I could feel it. Something was very, very wrong.

"We always do an X-ray," he said. "Procedure."

I had a choice. I could acquiesce and probably die in X-ray or I could flee convention and maybe have a shot at staying alive.

"You're fired," I said, choking on my ragged breathing. Oh, God, help me, I prayed. Help me keep my wits about me. Help me to *think for myself even though I don't know what's going on!*

They brought in a doctor from another hospital. He took one look at me. "This is not asthma!" he exploded. "It's anaphylactic shock!"

Everything went into high gear. An EKG was set up. Someone gave me an injection for my heart. Now something to relax what was apparently my uterus cramping—a common experience for women in anaphylactic shock. My doctor in Seattle was called. Finally, when I at last stabilized, the man who saved my life took my hand. "You got grit," he told me. "Anybody else would have folded."

I started to thank him, but he interrupted. "No, you've got nobody to thank but yourself. Nobody could have done what you did tonight. You were dying, and you were dying fast. And yet you had the courage to fire the only doctor around because you trusted yourself."

It was two o'clock in the morning when I let myself in through the back door. The house was quiet. My children had put themselves to bed. How close had their mother come to going out for a jog and never coming home? I pulled off my bloodied tights and my sweat-soaked shirt and tossed my inhaler into the drawer. I was alive—that was what counted. I ran a cool rag over my face. I was only alive, though, because I'd had the courage to defy a stupid doctor and to go ahead on my own, trusting in God to see me through.

I slid into bed, almost too weary and weak to pull up the covers. I soon fell asleep, though, for I'd learned, like the woman Christ healed by the touch of his robe, that God is with us whenever we have to make the Pilgrim's necessary and sometimes frightful journey—of flight and quest.

JANIE

O Lord, you have searched me
and you know me.
You know when I sit and when I rise;
you perceive my thoughts from afar.
You discern my going out and my lying down;
you are familiar with all my ways.
Before a word is on my tongue
you know it competely, O Lord.

—Psalm 139:1–4 (NIV)

The Pilgrim seeks to find that which God knows, and in *Their Eyes Were Watching God* Janie set out to do just that. The story opens with the end of her quest. She is walking back into town on a hot, Georgia night, her long hair tied into a ponytail and swinging down her back. The old ladies are out on their porches. Why's she wearing them overalls? Where's the blue satin dress? What happened to Tea Cake, that "lad" she run off with? Must have took all her money. Serves her right. Should have stayed in her class, she should.

Janie's quest had begun years before when at sixteen she felt, inside, answers seeking her out. She had only questions. What was love? Bees buzzed in her grandmother's blossoming pear trees. Will pears, she wondered, ever bloom for me? Will bees ever buzz?

Two marriages and the bees didn't sing. Nearly forty years old and she was a "rut in the road," "beaten down by the wheels."[12] She got from Jody Starks only what money could buy and she wondered if maybe Jody Starks was nothing, for all his talk and prestige as a store owner. But then, she decided, she'd have to lie and say he was, or life would be nothing but a house and a store.

But then Jody died and Tea Cake pranced and Janie's world was turned upside down. Tea Cake loved her. Tea Cake teased her. Tea Cake played with her and planted with her and laughed with her and talked to her. But Tea Cake was only thirty, Janie was nearly forty, and it wasn't fitting. But Janie heard the bees singing, and she bought a blue satin dress and married him anyway.

Their Eyes Were Watching God is the story of Janie's pilgrimage into answers for questions she'd had all her life, discovering in the process her own power to love and be loved—possible only because Tea Cake allowed her to be herself, to think her own thoughts, to make her own choices, to do what she wanted to do. "Ah wuz fumblin' round," she told him, "and God opened de door." Tea Cake died after they'd been together for only two years, but Janie came home to the store knowing who she was in God's eyes—and with a few answers.

Love wasn't a grindstone, she'd discovered, doing the same thing everywhere and with everyone it touched. She spoke to Phoeby, an old friend who'd come by with some mulatto rice to kill the "hongries." Phoeby would take the news back to the other ladies on their porches where they waited, wanting to hear of Janie's defeat. But Janie, pilgrimage complete, had not been defeated by flight and quest. She now knew what God knew. Love, she told Phoeby, was more like the sea, moving, taking its shape from the shore it meets, and different with every shore. And, she said, rice easing the hungries, Phoeby's companionship reaching out to her beyond the front porches, "You got tuh *go* there tuh *know* there. . . . Nobody else can't tell yuh and show yuh. Two things everybody's got tuh do fuh theyselves. They got tuh go tuh God, and they got tuh find out about livin' fuh theyselves."

If any of us are to ever hear the bees singing and find who we are in God's eyes, we have to take our journeys—like Janie—of flight and quest.

LAURA

"Do not give dogs what is sacred; do not throw your pearls to pigs. If you do, they may trample them under their feet, and then turn and tear you to pieces."

—*Matthew* 7:6 *(NIV)*

One rainy day a very spoiled little girl from Plum Creek came to visit at Laura Ingalls's house. After tearing the paper dolls in half, naughty Anna snatched Laura's rag doll and tugged on the shoe-button eyes, pulled on the braids, and even banged the doll's face on the floor. Horrified, Laura could do nothing. Anna was the "company" and Charlotte, after all, was only a doll. When it was time to go home, Anna threw a temper tantrum and insisted on taking Charlotte, and Laura was forced to "make the company happy" and to give up the doll.

"For shame, Laura," said Ma. "A great big girl like you sulking about a rag doll. Stop it, this minute. You don't want that doll, you hardly ever played with it. You must not be so selfish."[13]

She didn't want her doll? But of course she wanted her doll! But if she wanted her doll, then that would mean she was selfish! But she didn't want to be selfish! So that meant she *didn't* want her doll!

Right?

Growing up is hard, and this is why so many of us stop thinking for ourselves. Rather than think of ourselves as selfish, we deny who we are and what we want. We *don't* want Charlotte.

A few weeks later Laura found Charlotte drowned and frozen in a puddle: her doll had been thrown away and forgotten. Seeing her beloved Charlotte drowned and frozen caught Laura in crisis of contradiction. To complicate everything, not only did she *not want* Charlotte, Charlotte wasn't even her doll anymore. To her way of thinking, to rescue Charlotte was tantamount to stealing it. To reclaim it would defy what people expected of her. By the laws of Ma and Pa she was to walk away.

But how could she? How could she walk away and leave Charlotte? Contradiction comes to us even as children—and we have to choose. Are we going to start thinking for ourselves and be true to what we want—even at the risk of being called selfish? Or are we going to hold fast to our teachings and leave Charlotte behind?

Laura chose to be true to herself. She snatched up her doll, hid it under her shawl, and, frightened, ran panting home. "It's Charlotte," she told her mother. "I-I stole her. I don't care Ma, I don't care if I did!"[14]

Laura was fortunate. She lived with parents who weren't afraid of their mistakes. Ma sat Laura up on her knee, soothed back her hair, and invited Laura to tell her all about it—and they decided it had been a terrible experience for Charlotte, but that Laura had rescued her and now Ma would make her as good as new.

Some of us aren't so lucky. We live with those who maintain rigid positions, who deny us the right to make choices and to seek what we need and want. But it *is* still our choice. A replica of Laura's Charlotte sits on my bookshelf, reminding me that I can always choose, if I need to, the Pilgrim's path of flight and quest.

JOY

> *For we must all appear before the judgment seat of Christ, that each one may receive what is due him for the things done while in the body, whether good or bad.*
>
> —*2 Corinthians 5:10* (NIV)

Joy Johnson was head nurse on her floor at Vancouver General Hospital, a job everyone wanted. She'd made it up through bed care and into top-level management. Her hours were eight to five, she got great vacations, and received a top-dollar salary—not something easily accomplished for someone only thirty-six years old.

But then divorce rocked the boat.

"I was forced to really think about what I was doing," she said outside of a beach home she shares with her parents in Tsawwassen, B.C., Canada. "I was driving an hour each way into Vancouver, never saw the kids, and, worse, was taking the dreadful worries from the job home with me. Suddenly, the glamorous job wasn't so glamorous anymore."

She was offered work at the new, local hospital—but not in administration. "It was bed care," she said. "Hard work, changing shifts, lower pay, a drop in prestige. Everything I'd worked so hard for would no longer be mine. I almost didn't take it. But then I had to ask, 'What is my primary responsibility in life?' I looked at my two kids and knew the answer."

The choice was a difficult one. People don't back down career ladders, they climb them, and friends couldn't understand. But Joy kept thinking about Judgment Day and Christ asking, "What did you do with the responsibilities I gave you? What about Ryan and Christa?"

"It's really hard," she said, "when you think so differently from everyone else. I finally had to listen to myself and not worry about what anyone else thought. Life, for me right now, is making sure my kids get the attention and care they need. And so I took the plunge—and took the job just up the road." She laughed. "All my nursing points, I don't think, are going to impress God—not when all is said and done!"

Flight and quest. Fleeing the ideals of society in order to carve out your own. Joy is right; it's not an easy thing to do, and you sometimes wonder if you've done the right thing. "But you know," said Joy, gazing for a long time over the water and the distant peak of Mt. Baker in Washington state. "It *has* turned out so well. I used to think regular hours were an advantage, but I'm not sure why I ever thought that. I can go to parent/teacher conferences now. I can see the kids' school plays or go watch Ryan's baseball games. I just trade shifts with someone else. I couldn't do that working eight to five!

"No," she said, "sometimes the world doesn't see it the same way you do. But the way I look at it, God has given me Ryan and Christa, and there *is* a Judgment Day—and I want to stand proud of my accomplishments, in what counts."

She will, for when we seek only to answer to him, he always honors our Pilgrim's path of flight and quest.

DANIELLE

Trust in the Lord with all your heart
and lean not on your own understanding;
in all your ways acknowledge him,
and he will make your paths straight.

—*Proverbs 3:5, 6 (NIV)*

Success stories abound. All the world loves a winner, but what happens when we fail?

Danielle[15] studied opera for seven years, singing nationally and climbing her way to the top while holding down a full-time career job as manager of a large clothing store in southern California. At thirty years of age she succumbed to the still small voice that urged her to seek broader possibilities with her music. She quit her job and headed for Germany, alone, where she hoped to gain the required European experience to "make it big."

"I quit my job," she said, "because I asked myself the question, 'When I'm old, will I have lived the life I wanted to live? Will I be satisfied?' But when I got to Germany, I found I didn't like it. It rained all the time. It was depressing. I was competing against the same people I'd competed against before. I missed the States. And I found out that to be in opera you have to like to eat and talk singing. I like to eat and talk singing, but I also like other things."

So she came home. There are some who might criticize her quest, her leap into such a risky venture as opera, where only a handful of people ever make it to the top. She might be written up as having failed. After all, she didn't make it.

But Bruce Larson would not call her a failure. "A healthy person is someone who can choose risk and danger," he says in *There's a Lot More to Health Than Not Being Sick.*[16] He reminds us of the world-renowned Flying Wallendas aerial troupe. They were most famous for their human pyramid, balancing on a high wire with no net. Two men, standing on a thin wire, held a pole that, before it was over, held ten other people. One day it all came down in a small Midwestern town. Two were killed, two others maimed for life. A few days later, though, the Wallendas were back on the wire. When asked by reporters later why, Papa Wallenda responded without a moment's hesitation. "To be on the wire is life. All else is waiting."

Danielle came home to southern California and got back up on the wire. She began to sing and manage clothing shops and over the last several years has managed to creatively combine her dual talents, picking up where she left off and moving forward in both directions with an astonishing degree of success. She's sung opera in Washington, D.C., Philadelphia, Chicago, New York—all over the country. And her other business? She now owns a small chain of her own clothing stores.

"By faith," says Bruce Larson, "we can try to determine what God is up to with us, and fling our lives with reckless abandon into the causes we think He has for us."[17] We can fling, because when we listen to God's call, we cannot fail. Like Danielle, we learn more of who we are, pick up where we left off, and carry on. God uses our "failure" to bring about the bigger and better in our lives, and this is the wonderful truth of daring a Pilgrim's flight and quest.

$\mathcal{D}$ISCOVERING OURSELVES
The Bad and the Ugly, But Did We Forget the Good?

Search me, O God, and know my heart!
Test me and know my anxious thoughts!
See if there is any offensive way in me,
and lead me in the way everlasting!

—*Psalm 139:23, 24 (NIV)*

"We're off to see the Wizard," the Scarecrow and Dorothy sing, ready to launch upon their quest "the wonderful Wizard of Oz." But wait, the Scarecrow can't stay on his feet. Dorothy picks him up and sets him on his way. Down he falls again, up again she scoops him, until at last, tripping and slipping, he tumbles his way down the yellow brick road. When we first begin the Pilgrim's quest, we, like the Scarecrow, trip. Not used to thinking or acting on our own behalf, we aren't always sure about our decisions, nor do we always make those decisions gracefully. We wobble. We fall flat on our face. We even, as did the Scarecrow down the road a bit, get angry—explosively so.

Carol Pearson points out in *The Hero Within* that Pilgrims have usually "gone along with someone else, over their own wishes, too long, so that their resentment is deep by the time they act in their own interest. The result is that they choose themselves in the midst of a veritable explosion of rage."[18] Let's go back to *The Wizard of Oz* and look at the Scarecrow, who, up until now we've thought to be really rather nice. He and Dorothy have come to the apple orchard. Dorothy picks up an apple, but a tree gets mad—and so does the Scarecrow.

"Come along, Dorothy," he says, all wobbly on his feet and glaring furiously at the crabby apple tree, "you don't want any of *those* apples!"

"Are you hinting my apples aren't what they ought to be?" says the tree.

"Oh no!" the Scarecrow says, na-na-na-na-na-na in his voice. "It's just that she doesn't like eating little green worms!"

Anger. And it can scare those of us made of "sugar and spice and everything nice" right back up the Scarecrow post. Anger frightens us, badly, particularly our own, and we'd really rather forget our quest than risk such rage. I know I would. I get into a lot of trouble when I mouth off.

Yet, and I have to remind myself of this, was not Christ, at times, angry? Once he cursed a fig tree—for not bearing fruit. He often addressed the Pharisees with a cutting edge of sarcasm. Enraged, he one day drew a whip and sent it cracking, upsetting tables and bird cages and cow stalls and creating panic on the Temple steps. Yet the Bible tells us he was without sin.

Anger is not sin. Anger is part of the human experience. Furthermore, anger is a signal—and one worth listening to, says Dr. Harriet Goldhor Lerner in *The Dance of Anger.* "Our anger," she writes, "may be a message that we are being hurt, that our rights are being violated, that our needs or wants are not being adequately met, or simply that something is not right."[19]

What was wrong in Oz was that Dorothy was hungry, and there was no reason why the tree shouldn't have given her an apple to eat. Yet if the Scarecrow had denied his anger ("You're right, she keeps forgetting she's not in Kansas, we'll just mosey on our way, anything you say, Sir!"), Dorothy would have gone hungry. Likewise, whenever any of us deny our anger (because we don't like it or are afraid of it), we miss the opportunity to correct what's really wrong. Like the Scarecrow, we have to ask, *Why* am I angry? Is some basic right being violated? Is anyone being hurt? Am *I* being hurt? Is a need going unmet? It becomes the Pilgrim's task to figure it out and do something about it. Which is exactly what the Scarecrow did.

"I'll show you how to get apples," he hisses to Dorothy, sticking his thumb to his nose. "Na-na-na-na-na-na!" And in come the apples, bouncing and rolling all over the yellow brick road and into the woods beyond.

Several years ago only weeks after my ex-husband and I had separated, he let himself into the house without a word and out again with the TV, stereo, silver, and bank records. I stood at the door raw with rage and screamed my fury into the night. The echo of it still rings in my ears.

"Mummy," my six-year-old daughter said, starting to cry, a few moments later when I trembled up the stairs to tuck her into bed, "you were so angry."

Angry? I'd scared myself, I was so angry. But yet, anger is a signal. King David wrote in the Psalms: *Search me, O God, and know my heart! Try me and know my thoughts! And see if there be any wicked way in me, and lead me in the way everlasting!* The temptation here is to name our anger as the wicked within us. This is the most obvious. Yet David was not speaking of anger. He couldn't have; there is plenty of record documenting God's wrath, both God the Father's and God the Son's. Nor was he talking about our fumbling efforts to learn to control our anger. God himself often repented of his own wrath. Rather, David was speaking of something far more subtle, and far more serious. He was inviting God to search *beyond* the anger (and confusion and doubt and fear and all the other emotions we run into when we first start listening to ourselves) to see past the immediate and obvious *into the deeper issue.*

That night I had to burn the midnight oil. Search me, O God, and know my heart. Why had I gotten so enraged? Was I selfish? Undisciplined? I had to ask myself the hard questions. And when we ask the hard questions we sometimes discover things about ourselves we don't like very much—the bad and the ugly. In Walt Disney's movie version of *Pinocchio* when the little "wooden head" looked into the mirror, he certainly discovered for himself what a "jackass" he could be, and I, looking in a similar mirror of introspection, didn't like much of what I saw either. It was not the loss of "stuff" that had enraged me. It was that my ex-husband had not spoken to me while removing the "stuff." It was the disrespect that had set me off. But who's fault was that? I had to ask myself. Another tough question. For I had, as Dr. James Dobson puts it in *Love Must Be Tough,* too long allowed my marriage partner "to crawl all over the 'line of respect.'"[20] I had communicated, persistently and consistently down through the years, the message that I was not worth very much of anything, let alone explanation.

I was, in fact, a real wimp and the reality is, if you tell this to people long enough they'll start to believe it. I had no one to blame but myself.

Not all we discover about ourselves is bad and ugly, however. Sometimes we discover *good* things too and that night I found something good about myself. My ex-husband had taken my children's only form of entertainment. Hours, they'd spent, listening to their records, and this was what had really made me mad. He was stepping on their toes. If I was slow in drawing the line of respect when it came to myself, I was not, I also realized, slow when it came to my kids. I was not a total wimp; there was hope.

I would not have known this, though, had I not listened to the "signal" Dr. Lerner speaks of, and had instead spent the entire night beating myself over the head with the almighty guilt stick. As it was, Dr. Lerner's probing questions and God's nonjudgmental searching brought the deeper issues to light and in what was left of the night I was able to figure out how I was going to begin living my life as if it mattered and was worthy of consideration—and figure a way to meet the unmet needs of my children.

In the morning I called their father and explained why they needed their record player. He was more than willing to accommodate. It had not occurred to him the children used the stereo. He certainly didn't intend to "step" on anyone's "toes." That same week he brought over a new record player, one that suited their needs just fine, and I, like the Scarecrow, learned something important. By not letting my anger immobilize me with guilt, *I could get the apples!*

Not that anger gives us license to be childish and thumb our noses "Na-na-na-na-na-na!" whenever we don't get our own way or to be vulgar and fly off at the mouth in a manner that scares everyone around us, including ourselves. It does mean, though, we can accept anger into our lives for what it is, a signal that something is wrong—so we can do something about it.

In William Gibson's play *The Miracle Worker,* Annie Sullivan is warned before she leaves to work with Helen Keller that the child was "prone to temper tantrums."

"It only means," Annie promptly responded, "there is something inside trying to get out."

Our anger is a healthy indication that the real us is trying to speak.

Rome was not built in a day, though, and neither are we. We do not, as Carol Pearson points out, learn our lessons all at once.[21] Do you remember the bumper sticker? With the disordered alphabet? PBP, GINFWMY. Please Be Patient, God Is Not Finished With Me Yet. We have to be patient when we trip over our rage, and all the other emotions we stumble into; because—

By listening to our feelings we learn who we really are. The Scarecrow couldn't scare crows—but when he got mad he could *think!* He could get the apples. Which was significant, considering he wasn't supposed to have any brains.

What of Hagar, of the Old Testament? Son dying, water gone, she sat down and wept. Openly and unabashedly she admitted to emotions that ran the full gambit: uncertainty, fear, anxiety, loneliness, anger. What an honest, refreshing thing to do! She wept! And look what happened. Because she wept, because she dared to listen and honor her emotions, as negative as they were, God met her again and reaffirmed who she was. Tears reminded her that she was the mother of a nation: one who has seen God—and lived.

Our Pilgrim's journey is one of flight, and quest. We flee the expectations others have placed upon us, to quest our own identity. Wobbly on our feet and not used to thinking for ourselves, we fumble and fall and at times slam right up against a wall of rage—and fear and doubt and loneliness and anxiety and numerous other emotions that beset human beings engaged in the act of thinking. But these emotions, if we can look beyond their reality to why they exist, help us see more clearly who we are, which is what the role of Pilgrim is all about.

And once we know who we are, we are ready for the next step of our inner journey: Martyrdom.

"A Tinman!" exclaims Dorothy, apples in Oz all but forgotten in new discovery. The Tinman mumbles, mouth rusted shut, and both Dorothy and the Scarecrow rush to hear what he is saying. He wants the oil can.

They waste no time oiling first his mouth, squirting here, squirting there, now the knee, the foot. "Well, you're perfect now," announces Dorothy.

But no. The Tinman has no heart.

The poor Tinman. He thought he could be sort of human if only he . . . He breaks into song, dancing with a clinkety-clank-clank, bang, toot-toot! Dorothy whispers to the Scarecrow, the Scarecrow smiles. Oops, the Tinman trips. He staggers to the side of the yellow brick road. Dorothy sits beside him and sidles in close. She gives him another squirt.

"We were just wondering if you couldn't come with us," she asks and the Scarecrow nods, "to the Emerald City to ask the Wizard of Oz for a heart?"

Flight and quest. The Pilgrim comes full circle. Once fleeing everyone else's expectations we come back into the community—with purpose both for ourselves—and others. And ready to meet the Tinman so that we might learn the task of what it means to be a Martyr, to give of our self to help someone else.

NOTES

1. Tim Hansel, *You Gotta Keep Dancin'* (Elgin, IL: David C. Cook, 1985), 41.

2. Quoted by James M. Houston, "The Independence Myth," *Christianity Today,* 15 January 1990, 32.

3. Bruce Larson, *Ask Me To Dance* (Waco, TX: Word Books, 1972), 16.

4. John Bunyon, *The Pilgrim's Progress* (Old Tappan, NJ: Revell, 1977), 13–15.

5. Elizabeth Deen, *All the Women of the Bible* (San Francisco: Harper & Row, 1955), 111.

6. Deen, *All the Women of the Bible,* 110.

7. Elizabeth Cady Stanton, "Declaration of Sentiments" in Susan B. Anthony and Melissa Joslyn Gage, eds., *History of Woman Suffrage* (New York: Flower & Wells, 1881), 70.

8. Lois Banner, "Elizabeth Cady Stanton: Early Marriage and Feminist Rebellion," Linda K. Kerber and Jane DeHart-Mathews, eds. *Women's America* (New York: Oxford University Press, 1987), 209.

9. Banner in Kerber and DeHart-Mathews, eds., *Women's America,* 203.

10. Stanton in Anthony & Gage, eds., *History of Woman Suffrage,* 71.

11. John 12:7 (KJV).

12. Zora Neale Hurston, *Their Eyes Were Watching God* (Philadelphia: J.B. Lippincott, 1937, renewed 1965 by John C. Hurston and Joel

Hurston. Reprinted by permission of HarperCollins Publishers), 118, 236, 285.

13. Laura Ingalls Wilder, *On The Banks of Plum Creek* (New York: Harper & Row, 1971), 232.

14. Wilder, *Plum Creek,* 236.

15. Not her real name.

16. Bruce Larson, *There's A Lot More To Health Than Not Being Sick* (Waco, TX: Word, 1981), 78.

17. Larson, *More To Health Than Not Being Sick,* 81.

18. Carol Pearson, *The Hero Within* (San Francisco: Harper & Row, 1986), 64.

19. Harriet Goldhor Lerner, *The Dance of Anger* (New York: Harper & Row, 1985), 1.

20. James C. Dobson, *Love Must Be Tough* (Waco, TX: Word, 1983), 88.

21. Pearson, *The Hero Within,* 63.

FIVE MARTYR

"I can subdue this dragon through sacrifice."

—*Ruth the Martyr*

CHOOSING TO SACRIFICE
From A Position of Power

"Don't urge me to leave you or to turn back from you. Where you go I will go, and where you stay I will stay. Your people will be my people and your God my God. Where you die I will die, and there I will be buried. May the Lord deal with me, be it ever so severely, if anything but death separates me from you." When Naomi realized that Ruth was determined to go with her, she stopped urging her.

—*Ruth 1:16–18 (NIV)*

The wicked Witch of the West explodes from her sulphur ball atop the roof of a cabin alongside the yellow brick road. We *all* gasp. Beside me my youngest son, Blake, cowers, hiding his face from the hatred that twists the features of a witch who personifies all our worst fears.

"Stay away from Dorothy!" the wicked witch screeches, her long and bony finger jabbing the air. She threatens to make a mattress out of the Scarecrow and turn the Tinman into a beehive if they don't mind their own business, and to prove herself perfectly capable she throws down a fireball, aimed straight for the Scarecrow's feet. Up he jumps, yelping and dancing, flames leaping high, and we gasp again. But then the Tinman falls over the fire and douses the flames with his hat. Without thinking twice he saves the Scarecrow's life at risk to his own. We all draw a long sigh of relief and Blake sits up straight.

There is redemption in suffering and sacrifice. The Tinman, the Martyr in *The Wizard of Oz,* instinctively knows this—as do we all. Even the early fertility religions understood the mysterious relationship between sacrifice and redemption. Ishtar (or Innana), the earliest recorded spiritual deity, sacrificed her shepherd son/lover,

Damuzi, each year so the crops might flourish, and in various re-ligions since some form of this redemptive suffering has been critical. In Christianity God himself is our sacrifice.

However, women in our culture are often squeezed into a suf-fering role to the exclusion of other options. When we do not understand choice in the face of conflict, martyrdom becomes our standard response. As a result we often wind up like poor Cinder-ella of the fairy tales, a servant in our own home, on the job, or even down at the PTA.

There is a somber tone to the music when the storybook opens in Walt Disney's movie version of *Cinderella*. Silhouetted against the opaque sky is a turreted mansion fallen into disrepair. The camera rolls in and we hear, "Take that ironing and have it back in an hour. *One hour,* you hear?"

"Don't forget the mending. Don't be all day getting it done—either!"

"Pick up the laundry and get on with your duties."[1]

"Cinderella!"

"Cinderella!"

"CINDERELLA!"

Sadly, like Cinderella, we often do the ironing, mending, and laundry in the hopes that our suffering might ultimately bring us the love and redemption we seek. What those of us who do this don't understand is that *suffering doesn't always bring redemption*—which is why the dragons often triumph and step-mothers reign.

An employee gives up supper hours and weekends and wonders why the boss doesn't reward her. Mothers sacrifice time and self and wonder why children show no respect. Wives deny their own interests and identity and wonder why husbands don't appreciate or love them. When there is no balance of self and sacrifice, the more we give the less we receive—and, sadly, there is often se-rious abuse for our trouble. The harsh reality is that some people like to watch a martyr cut herself into pieces—and then treat her accordingly.

The large cupboard, clean it! Windows upstairs and downstairs, wash them! The tapestries and the draperies, shake them!

"But I already—"

Do them again! And weed the garden, scrub the terrace, sweep the halls, sweep the stairs, clean the chimneys, and of course there's the mending and sewing and laundry! And don't forget the cat! Bathe him!

"Yes, ma'am."

Jesus Christ reminds us this is *not* what the role of Martyr is all about. Martyrdom, he says, is a choice—something we, and Cinderella, have forgotten. When he saw the large crowd, "his heart was filled with pity for them, and he healed their sick."[2] Yet after healing a man of a crippled hand and the Pharisees made plans to kill Jesus, he heard of it and "went away from that place."[3] When four thousand gathered and there was nothing to eat, he fed them so they would not "faint as they go."[4] But when he fed five thousand people and they were ready to make him king, by force if necessary, he "went off again to the hills by himself."[5] When he was tired and the people brought their babies, the disciples scolded. Christ, though, said, "Let the children come to me!"[6] But when the teachers of the law asked for a miracle, he said, "No!"[7] Ultimately he sacrificed his life, but on his terms. "*I* lay down my life," he told his disciples, "that *I* may take it again. No one takes it from me, but *I* lay it down of my own accord. *I* have power to lay it down, and *I* have power to take it again."[8] There was no wicked stepmother calling the shots.

For those of us sitting by the hearth, though, it's not so easy to claim a choice. "What! *Not* clean out the cinders?" It feels selfish. After all, "I want to go to the ball!" is not something we're used to saying. But if we can plug our ears long enough to all the demands (Cinderella! *Cinderella! CINDERELLA!*) and open our eyes to Christ, the confusion clears.

Two conditions seemed to have guided him whenever he was up against the Martyr's choice. One, would the sacrifice forward his mission and enable him to complete the purpose for which he was sent? And two, would his sacrifice bring redemption for someone around him? If not, not even the authority of the church with all its reason and tradition could force him to submit. Martyrdom, he taught, is a *choice to redeem,* and it's based upon *who we are* and *what we are meant to do with our lives*—not mandate or guilt.

In the fairy tale *Cinderella,* word goes out that the duke is looking for the maid who fits the glass slipper. Drusella shoves an armful of ironing into Cinderella's face.

Anastasia throws another dress onto the pile in Cinderella's arms and spins about the room. "We've got to get dressed!"

But for the first time in her life, Cinderella hands the clothes back. WHAT? Stunned, Anastasia and Drusella watch as their step-sister floats, singing, from the room. Yes, dressed, she sings; it would never do for the duke to find her in rags.

Is our suffering compatible with what God has called us to do with our lives? And does our suffering bring redemption to those around us?

Cinderella finally figured out that sacrifice without choice is not redemptive but victimizing—for all concerned. And it's lucky for us she did. If she hadn't, she'd still be cleaning out cinders—and we wouldn't know that choice is what ultimately brings about the redemption we seek.

The story of Ruth in the Old Testament is the Bible's own fairy tale, and it provides us with a spiritual model of what it really means to be a Martyr. Once upon a time, as the story goes, in about the year 1100 B.C., there was famine in the kingdom and Elimelech and his wife took their two very handsome sons to sojourn in the nearby land of Moab. There they ate, drank, and were merry, and in time the two sons took unto themselves two very beautiful Moabite maidens as brides. For a while all was well, until one day tragedy struck. Elimelech died, and so did the sons. Only the three widows were left: the mother-in-law, Naomi, and the sisters-in-law, Orpah and Ruth. Now, Ruth and Orpah could return to their fathers and find protection, as was the custom of their land, but what of Naomi? Where was she to go? What was she to do?

Her only choice was a return to her own people in the kingdom, and because the daughters-in-law were so fond of her, they chose to go along. A few days into the journey, though, Naomi began to think better of it and begged her daughters-in-law to return. What future did they have? They were better off in Moab, where they might remarry, have children, and find happiness.

Oh, but Ruth and Orpah cried. Noami got stern. "No, my daughters, for it is exceedingly bitter to me for your sake that the hand of the Lord has gone forth against me!"

Finally Orpah, a bright and sensible girl, tearfully saw the sense of what Naomi was saying. Where she went, who would marry her?

No one. She'd be reduced to begging, an outcast of society in a foreign land. But in Moab, there was her own home, and time was not so far gone she could not remarry. She kissed her mother-in-law goodbye and slowly retraced her steps.

Now Ruth, on the other hand, clung to her mother-in-law and wept. She could not bear to see Naomi go on alone. What would Naomi do? There would be robbers on the way. And once in the kingdom, could an old woman glean the fields?

"See, your sister-in-law has gone back to her people and to her gods," said Naomi, pushing Ruth away as only an old woman can do. "Return after your sister-in-law."

"Oh, entreat me not," cried Ruth, "to leave you or to return from following you! For where you go I will go, and where you lodge I will lodge. Your people shall be my people, and your God my God. Where you die I will die, and there will I be buried. May the Lord do so to me and more also if even death parts me from you."

When Naomi saw that Ruth was determined, she said nothing more, and they made their way to the kingdom. There they met Boaz— And here I interrupt because here is redemptive sacrifice. Unlike the story of Cinderella, martyrdom was not exacted but voluntarily given, and the choice to suffer was motivated by a desire to ease a very real burden and not merely to cater to the whim or dictates of another. Furthermore, Ruth's decision was one of power. It was not as if she were destitute, with no place else to go. And because she chose, redemption was found. She and Boaz met, fell in love, married, and lived happily ever after.

Genuine sacrifice, Pearson reminds us in *The Hero Within,* is "transformative and not maiming."[9] It's respective of both giver and receiver.[10] Not that we all wind up marrying Boaz or Prince Charming, or even that our efforts are materially rewarded. But once we start to give honestly, out of a sense of who we are and what God has called us to be instead of out of guilt and someone else's demands, we find redemption at hand and the dragons backing down.

This cannot happen, though, until we first take the Pilgrim's journey. We can't make a choice to give of ourselves until we first know ourselves. And if we give only because we've been commanded to, or we feel guilty if we don't, or because we've been told that this is what we were created to do, we'll never understand what it means to redeem and save. We only perpetrate dysfunction and abuse, we find no healing or growth or hope. We lose more of who we are and we drift further from what God intended us to be. But! If Martyrdom is a choice based from a position of power and clear identity—in order to redeem and save, we discover very quickly that we can't outgive. We regain what we sacrifice, in twice and thrice the measure. Christ said, "For whoever would save his life will lose it; and whoever loses his life for my sake and the gospel's will save it,"[11]and it's the martyr, not the victim, who discovers this to be true.

In *The Wizard of Oz* the Tinman certainly discovers this to be true. Right after he puts out the fire and everyone has caught their breath, he declares to Dorothy, "I'll see you reach the Wizard, whether I get a heart or not." He doesn't care what he might gain, he only wants to give, and while he may not have thought he had a heart he seems instinctively to know that to give his heart, his life, is to gain it. And is this not what happened? By taking Dorothy to the Wizard, he receives all that he asks for—and more.

Yet it was his choice to give of himself, or not to give. It was his choice because he knew who he was—or rather who he was *not*. "Beehive! Bah-a! Let her try," he'd said, "to make a beehive out of me!"

Martyrdom is not an automatic response based on powerlessness and victimization, for that is only Cinderella at the hearth. Rather, it's a choice for redemptive sacrifice, based on a position of power. It's Cinderella going to the ball, handing back the ironing and mending. It's Ruth, going with her mother-in-law to a new land. And it's the Tinman taking Dorothy to find the wonderful Wizard of Oz.

It's the Pilgrim who has at last come to know who she is.

BRENDA

Each one must do as he has made up his mind, not reluctantly or under compulsion, for God loves a cheerful giver.

—*2 Corinthians 9:7 (rsv)*

My panda bear begged me not to give him up, but in the back of my mind my Sunday school teacher's voice quietly argued, "We never give away what we don't need anymore, for then it's not sacrificial. We only give God our very best and that which we love the most." I could feel hot tears burn behind my eyes. I was five years old and the fire department was collecting old toys for poor children that Christmas in 1957.

I could hear my mother down the hall, hurrying my sisters along. They seemed to have no problem bundling up comic books, plastic baby bottles, a few dolly dresses, cutouts, and storybooks. Their unperturbed chatter only made my agony more private. Someone please stop me, I cried—even as I bundled Panda into a blanket. Please . . .

"Are you sure you want to take your bear?" my mother asked, standing at the door, my jacket in her hand. My mother was a woman who got upset when people gave missionaries old tea bags.

"Yes," I said.

We drove to the city hall and got out. Firemen were directing mothers and fathers to drop the toys in big buckets or put things on a large table. My feet stopped and my younger sister bumped into me, plowing me down.

"Go ahead, lay it right there. My, what a nice little bear," the man said. Numb, I laid Panda on top of a rusty truck. God? *God!* Panda was grayish white and navy blue. My heart hurt when I looked at his navy blue eye. But then a lady with an orange hat dumped a stack of boys' toys on top of Panda and my mother was dragging me back down to the car. Panda? Panda! PANDA BEAR! But I didn't cry, even though something was wrong, horribly wrong, and trees zipped past the window, carrying me far, far away from . . .

For years I didn't cry for Panda. I couldn't. To cry would mean I was sorry I'd given him away, that I was selfish.

Ten years later, for something to do during the long lonely nights we lived in Iowa, I pieced together a doll from my mother's scrap bag in the back of the closet under the stairs. McCall (for so she was called, since I'd created her from a pattern I'd found in a McCall's magazine) was made of unbleached muslin. Her hair, soft brown yarn, was looped all curly and cute and stitched by hand onto her head. Shoebuttons polished with vaseline were her eyes. I embroidered with floss, eyebrows, a tiny little mouth, and a wee little nose. Her wardrobe rivaled Queen Elizabeth's. I sewed a tartan winter coat with little pockets and a matching hat with a bright red pom-pom and matching red ribbons to tie beneath her chin. I made flannel nighties, pretty dresses with lace, undershirts that snapped on, a dozen diapers, jumpers, overalls, T-shirts, and even a pair of denim jeans. I knit sweaters, more dresses, pantaloons, booties and mittens, and a scarf to match the coat. I patchworked a blanket and made two receiving blankets, and by spring she'd become my child; and my family, as was our summer custom during those years, headed for Boundary Bay and my grandfather's beach house just outside of Vancouver, B.C., Canada.

I took McCall with me, and while I do not remember exactly when I took it into my head to give her away, by the time we'd reached the little cabin I knew I would. But to whom, I wondered, was I going to give her?

As a child I'd grown up hearing all about the Joneses, the Pattersons, and the Slaneys—missionaries my folks supported—and that summer the Pattersons, missionaries from Japan, were on furlough. They arrived at the Bay and I took one look at the little girl, the youngest of five, and pulled out the gift I'd spent an entire winter making.

"Are you sure you want to give away your doll?" my mother asked. This time I did not hear my Sunday school teacher's voice or envision old tea bags. I saw only the little girl, my own heart, and nodded yes.

What was the difference between Panda and McCall? So often when we read 2 Corinthians 9:7 we interpret it under the lamp of guilt. We see it as a command, and because we don't want to be "disobedient," we pull ourselves up by the bootstraps, slap a cheery smile on our face, give away our hearts, and then wonder why we hurt so badly inside.

But is this verse a command? *Each one must do as he has made up his mind.* This doesn't sound much like an order to me, more like choice.

At five years old I was propelled by an overactive sense of obligation, not choice. At fifteen, though, I was propelled by a compelling sense of choice, not obligation—and this is the difference. Unfortunately, a lot of us never get past being five years old and the crippling burden of guilt. There comes a time, however, when we have to grow up. It *is* our choice, and no matter how hard we try to be cheerful, unless the decision comes from our own minds (and hearts), it will tear us apart every single time.

There are times when I still cry for Panda. But McCall? There is no room for regret, when the choice for martyrdom is truly ours.

MARY

> *"This is my commandment, that you love one another as I have loved you. Greater love has no man than this, that a man lay down his life for his friends."*
>
> —*John 15:12, 13 (RSV)*

The Puritans, fleeing religious persecution in England, came to the American colonies to preach religious freedom, yet in that "freedom" they committed unspeakable horrors against the Quakers. In a text we don't often read in the study of our history, we come to words too shy to speak full truth:

> William Brend, though the oldest of the band of missionaries, was called to pass through the most cruel sufferings that were meted out in Boston to any prisoner. The tale is too awful to tell in detail, but the inhumanity can be judged from the fact that one incident in his round of torture consisted of one hundred and seventeen blows on his bare back with a tarred rope. He was found dying—"his body having turned cold" and "his flesh having rotted". . . John Norton, however, was still

stout in his remorseless attitude, saying of William Brend: "He endeavored to beat the gospel ordinances black and blue, and it was but just to beat him black and blue."[12]

Things deteriorated quickly in Boston. Quakers were fined in excess of £1,000, their children were sold, their ears were cut off, holes were bored through their tongues, they were imprisoned without food or heat, they were chained to logs, they were laid neck and heels in irons, they were publicly whipped, H's were burnt into their hands, their appeals to England were denied, their houses and land were seized, atrocities culminating until, finally, in 1658, the clergy of the Massachusetts Colony executed a law that, after railing and abuse against the Quakers, stated:

> "And the said person, being convicted to be of the sect of the Quakers, shall be sentenced to banishment, *upon pain of death.*"[13]

The test wasn't long in coming. August 1659, Mary Dyer, a Quaker minister, went to Boston to request a repeal. She was apprehended, tried, and banished *upon pain of death.* But the day she was released, Christopher Holder, a colleague, was also apprehended and imprisoned. Mary Dyer turned right around and went back.

This time two men, William Robinson and Marmeduke Stephenson, joined her. All three were brought before the General Court October 19, 1659, and asked by the Governor why they had come. To request the repeal, Mary stated again, of the unrighteous law, "in obedience to the call of the Lord." With that "affrontive" reply, Governor Endicott chose to back his edict.

"Hearken, you shall be led back to the place from whence you came and from thence to the place of execution," he thundered, "to be hanged on the gallows till you are dead!"

"The will of the Lord be done," said Mary Dyer quietly.

"Take her away, Marshall!" screamed Endicott.

"Yea, joyfully," said Mary, "shall I go."[14]

October 27, 1659, they were marched to the gallows, William, Marmeduke, Mary between them and all holding hands. "Are you not ashamed," an official accosted Mary, "to walk thus between two young men?"

"No, this is to me the hour of the greatest joy I ever had in this world."[15]

The men were hung first, then Mary took her place, arms bound, now legs, now the handkerchief laid over her face, and finally now the noose about her neck. Suddenly, "Reprieve!"

Actually, the Court had never intended to hang her. John Winthrop, Governor of Connecticut, had pleaded on his knees before the Boston magistrates not to hang the Quakers. They let him have Mary, with this order written into the records.

> It is ordered that the said Mary Dyer shall have liberty for forty-eight hours to depart out of this Jurisdiction, after which time, being found therein, she is to be forthwith executed. And it is further ordered that she shall be carried to the place of execution and there to stand upon the gallows with a rope about her neck until the Rest be executed; and then to return to the prison and remain as aforesaid.[16]

But Mary Dyer refused to accept her life—so long as the law of death against her people remained. She returned for a third time in May to appear before the next General Court.

"Are you the same Mary Dyer that was here before?" Governor Endicott asked.

"I am the same."

"You will own yourself a Quaker, will you not?"

"I own myself to be reproachfully so called."

"This is no more than what thou saidst before. But now, it is to be executed."

"I came in obedience to the will of God at your last General Court, desiring you to repeal your unrighteous laws of banishment on pain of death; and that same is my word now, and earnest request, although I told you that if you refused to repeal them, the Lord would send others of His servants to witness against them."[17]

One more time marched to the gallows, one more time arms bound, now feet, now noose about her neck. "We will not hang you," said the authorities, "if you will promise to go home, back to Rhode Island."

I wonder what her thoughts might have been. No one knows, but we do know what she said. "Nay, I cannot," she said, voice firm. "In obedience to the will of the Lord God I came and in His will I abide faithful to death."

Mary Dyer died that day in Boston, May 21, 1660. A minister of the Gospel, she chose to sacrifice herself that others might live. That day the governor and clergymen rejoiced, but the people who had witnessed the brutality did not. A petition was sent to England. Because of Mary Dyer, who committed herself thrice to die that others might live, religious persecution was immediately and henceforth stopped. By edict of King Charles.

Today a bronze statue of Mary Dyer stands on Boston's capitol grounds, within sight of the Commons where she was hung, a larger than life reminder to us all that there is always redemption in sacrifice, when, once, twice, thrice, the choice to give is ours.

RAHAB

By faith the prostitute Rahab, because she welcomed the spies, was not killed with those who were disobedient.

—*Hebrews 11:31* (NIV)

"Go get your mistress! Now." A loud, authoritative voice shot up the narrow passage from the main room of the inn below.

Upstairs, Rahab glanced at the two strange men seated at her table, then quickly out the window at soldiers' horses down below, almost lost in the dim light of waning day, impatiently pawing the dusty earth. "Who are you," she asked, "that the king's men come to my door?

"You're spies!" she cried almost immediately, panic in her eyes. "You're Israelites!"

The two men sprang to their feet, hidden knives drawn.

"No!" she cried. "Up to the roof! Quick!"

She hid them under stalks of drying flax and then, heart hammering, descended the narrow stairs. "Yes?" she asked, curtsying quickly before the soldiers. "I'm sorry to have kept you waiting. I was bathing. The evening, it is so hot . . . "

"Bring the men out," said the largest of the soldiers, a man she recognized, a man who played no games with his enemies.

"There are always men here," said Rahab, unwilling yet to make her choice. Should she risk her life? It wasn't too late. A nod of her head, and the hiding men were dead. But then, what of her family?

Surely they would perish, everyone of them, if the Israelites were to attack. "Men come and men go," she said, smiling sweetly.

"The foreigners. They arrived this morning. They were seen entering your inn."

"Wearing wool cloaks?" she queried, allowing a puzzled frown to come to her pretty face and glancing at the captain, tilting her head in the unspoken language of submission. "The men who spoke with a lilt in their voices?"

"The same," the captain grunted, thawing.

She tried a sorry smile. "They left at dusk," she whispered. "Yes, they wanted to know when the city gates were closed. Perhaps if you hurry," she said, smiling brightly now, "you can catch up with them?" And she set her chin to challenge.

She watched from the rooftop the slow swing of the gates as they opened out to the desert, spilling the king's fleet of horses and men into the night. Torchlights cast shadows across a moonless terrain.

"It's safe," she whispered, her heart only now slowing to a steady beat within her breast. "You can come out."

We know the rest of the story. Because she had faith in a God who'd parted the Red Sea and brought legendary victories to an untried army, she'd risked her life so that her family might be spared. "Please swear to me by the Lord," she told the spies even as they brushed off flax and scratched itchy skin, "that you will show kindness to my family, because I have shown kindness to you."[18]

"The city shall be accursed . . . " declared Joshua, the leader of the Israelite army, upon hearing of her bravery and choice. "Only Rahab the harlot shall live, she and all that are with her in the house, because she hid the messengers that we sent."[19]

Rahab reminds us that the choice for martyrdom, made in faith, can always be ours.

HARRIET

*You see, at just the right time, when we were still powerless,
Christ died for the ungodly. Very rarely will anyone die for a
righteous man, though for a good man someone might possibly
dare to die. But God demonstrates his own love for us in this:
While we were still sinners, Christ died for us.*

—Romans 5:6–8 (NIV)

"Hattie," wrote Harriet Beecher Stowe's sister-in-law from Boston
in 1850, "if I could use a pen as you can, I would write something
that will make this whole nation feel what an accursed thing slavery
is."[20]

Harriet read the letter in the sun room of her home, and then
glancing at her children busy with books and other occupations,
she started to tell them of the atrocities that were occurring under
the new Fugitive Slave Law. Suddenly she jumped to her feet impassioned
and, clutching the letter in her hand, she said, "I will
write something. I will—if I live."

But she didn't know what to write. For months she fretted. Her
husband left after Christmas for Cincinnati for three months.
"You'll think of it," he said, but two more months passed and
nothing. One Sunday in late February she was in church. Wind and
snow swept the window panes, the preacher's voice droned on
and on, and suddenly—a vision! An old black man, beaten and
tortured—by two other black men, urged on by a cruel slave master.
The dying man was to confess, but confess to what? Never
mind, thought Harriet. She would figure it out. For now she was
caught by the man's strength. Though whips tore at his back, pulling
out great chunks of flesh, he refused to cry out, to give in, and
when he neared his end, he looked up, and with great pity and
love in his face he forgave. The vision was of a black Christ, dying
for the sins of humanity. Martyrdom. What greater story could
there be? Harriet wondered, gathering her skirts and checking her
watch. When the last hymn was sung, she tied on her bonnet,
gathered her children, and hurried home.

All afternoon she wrote, using every scrap of writing paper she
had and then making do with brown paper that had wrapped the

groceries. The storm still howled, and still she wrote. Not until dinner was she done, pouring onto paper what has since become the famous martyr scene of *Uncle Tom's Cabin*. The scene completed, she arose, fixed a light supper, and gathered the children round to hear.

The children were in tears. "Oh, Ma! Slavery is the most cruel thing in the world!" the littlest child sobbed, and Harriet folded the manuscript, knowing she had her story at last.

But in the morning she felt differently. It was too harsh, too brutal. She put it away in a bedside bureau. When Calvin came home in March, he came out of the bedroom where he'd been rummaging about for some papers. His face was streaked in tears. He held out his wife's manuscript.

"Hattie, dear," he said, "this is your story. You must begin at once. Start at the beginning and work your way up to this. If you can do it, you'll have written the greatest story ever told."

Uncle Tom's Cabin did become the greatest story ever told in American literature. Politically, the book sparked the wrath of the North. Abraham Lincoln said, when meeting her, "So here's the little lady who started the big war," and it was he who credited her and "Uncle Tom" for swaying England to the side of the North in the Civil War. All around the world great leaders sought her out, and gifts from countries far and wide came in. In the literary world, Henry Wadsworth Longfellow, Charles Dickens, Heinrich Heine, Henry James, George Sand, John Greenleaf Whittier, Thomas Macaulay, and even Leo Tolstoy paid homage, declaring her work a mark of literary genius. In just four months Mrs. Stowe made ten thousand dollars, more money than her husband could have made in ten years. She went on to make hundreds of thousands of dollars, grossing more money than had ever been made before on a novel. The book was translated into forty languages and sold millions of copies all over the world. At one point nineteen companies performed the play on stage, sometimes as many as three shows a day, and it was the longest running play in American theater, *running uninterrupted for eighty-one years*.

For a time, though, the literary world forgot Harriet Beecher Stowe and her Uncle Tom. The writing was considered too "predictably religious" and heralded as sentimental drivel. But in recent years she has been rediscovered and is now recognized as one of the country's most gifted folklorists. Why?

Because Uncle Tom chose, like Christ, to die so that others might live. What was he being beaten for? What did Harriet "figure out"? He was to confess the whereabouts of two escaped slaves, but he wouldn't do it. And if the story has come back into its own, it's because martyrdom, as brutal and ugly and "predictably religious" as it is, always holds power—when the choice to give is ours.

JANE

Let him kiss me with the kisses of his mouth—
For your love is more delightful than wine.

—Song of Solomon 1:1a (NIV)

When Jane Eyre discovered on her wedding day that her groom was already married, and married to an insane woman at that, she fled Thornfield Hall. A distraught parting to be sure, and she nearly wavered. "Think of his misery," she cried unto herself. "Think of his danger—look at his state when left alone; remember his headlong nature; consider the recklessness following on despair—soothe him, save him, love him, tell him you love him and will be his."[21]

But how could she choose to sacrifice herself, when once she was "an ardent, expectant woman—almost a bride," but was now a "cold, solitary girl again"? The choice to redeem and save must come from a strong sense of Self, and this Jane Eyre no longer possessed.

We all know the story. She wandered the country for several days. St. John found her, his sisters nursed her back to health, and in her time with them came to discover more of her identity. She was their cousin for one thing. She was also a teacher. She was even rich, for she'd inherited unknown wealth. And a year after her flight from Thornfield she was also the object of St. John's designs. In June he proposed. Not because he loved her, but because she would make a "suitable helpmeet" on the mission fields of India.

She immediately objected on the grounds that she had no vocation for it. "I have," said he, "an answer for you—hear it." He went on to say how he'd studied her for ten months and how he'd found that she could "perform well, punctually, uprightly," and that he'd found in her the "complement of the qualities I seek." Namely, she was "docile, diligent, disinterested, faithful, constant and courageous; very gentle, and very heroic." Furthermore, it was God's will she do this. Her refusal could be nothing but a deliberate choice to deny God. In short, St. John tried to coerce from her a choice for Martyrdom so that his own needs might be met— with no consideration for her own.

Charlotte Bronte subtly points out several ironies here. First of all, St. John, for all his truth and perfection, did not love Jane, whereas Rochester, for all his deceit and homeliness, did. Second, the loveless marriage to a missionary was something society would approve of, whereas a loving marriage to Rochester was not. Third, while both men tried desperately to beg her hand in marriage, St. John tried to do it by "telling" her how things were going to be, Rochester asked. Fourth, St. John "told" Jane who she was, Rochester admitted he didn't know. And finally, when all was said and done, St. John did not allow Jane the choice to Martyr herself. Rochester did.

And Jane, thinking of St. John's proposal, realized, "No: such a martyrdom would be monstrous." God did not give her life to just throw it away, as surely she would if she married a man who could value her no more than a soldier might a good gun.

But Martyrdom to Rochester? Suddenly these ironies, standing back to back, prompted her to return to Thornfield, and Rochester. She was a different person, she knew more of herself, she was no longer cold and solitary. Perhaps . . . Well, she was just going to have to find out whether she would be of greater use remaining in England, or leaving it.

We know the ending. "Jane, will you marry me?"

"Yes, sir."

"A poor blind man, whom you will have to lead about by the hand?"

"Yes, sir."

"A crippled man, twenty years older than you, whom you will have to wait on?"

"Yes, sir."

"Truly, Jane?"

"Mr. Rochester, if ever I did a good deed in my life—if ever I thought a good thought—if ever I prayed a sincere and blameless prayer—if ever I wished a righteous wish—I am rewarded now. To be your wife is, for me, to be as happy as I can be on earth."

"Because you delight in sacrifice?"

"Sacrifice! What do I sacrifice? Famine for food, expectation for content. To be privileged to put my arms round what I value—to press my lips to what I love—to repose on what I trust: is that to make a sacrifice? If so, then certainly I delight in sacrifice."

Through Jane, one of the most loved women in all of English literature, certainly one of the most well-known, we learn there is nothing but delight in sacrifice—when the choice to give is ours.

LINDA

Jesus sat down opposite the place where the offerings were put and watched the crowd putting their money into the temple treasury. Many rich people threw in large amounts. But a poor widow came and put in two very small copper coins, worth only a fraction of a penny.

Calling his disciples to him, Jesus said, "I tell you the truth, this poor widow has put more into the treasury than all the others. They all gave out of their wealth; but she, out of her poverty, put in everything—all she had to live on."

—Mark 12:41–44 (NIV)

At the time of divorce a woman's standard of living decreases by 73 percent while a man's increases by 42 percent.[22] Can you imagine losing almost 75 percent of your current income? What would you do? You'd lose your home, your health, your peace of mind. Worse, and this is probably what cripples a single mother most, she loses her ability to give. So busy trying to keep food on the table, she has no money or time to spare.

When she turns to the Bible for comfort, it seems only to mock a pain that won't go away. What *can* she give? Even the poor widow in Mark had more than she. The widow at least had two copper coins to rub together.

Linda Whipple of Los Angeles was no different than any of the other twelve million single mothers in America.[23] Divorced and left with two children, one and three years old, she was caught in financial ruin. No money for rent, for food, for clothing. What could she give? "What I missed most," she says, "was not being able to give *anything*. I would look around . . . and nothing." What *is* there when you don't even have two copper coins worth a fraction of a penny?

But Linda Whipple found something she could give—her blood.

"It was my first attempt to give back," she says, and you can still hear the pain in her voice as she talks of those days. "I'm grateful to the Red Cross. They gave me an opportunity to give, to have a ministry."

For a long time this widow's mite was all Linda could give, until Fullerton Evangelical Free Church gave her a place of leadership under Gary Richmond, the country's only single-parent pastor, where she served as coordinator of the church's "Ounce of Prevention" program. If the Bible were being written today I suspect her name would be in its pages, for Linda Whipple reminds us all that no matter how poor we may be, we need not feel victimized. Martyrdom, the widow's mite, can still be ours to choose.

JUNE

. . . There was given me a thorn in my flesh, a messenger of Satan, to torment me. Three times I pleaded with the Lord to take it away from me. But he said to me, "My grace is sufficient for you, for my power is made perfect in weakness." Therefore I will boast all the more gladly about my weaknesses, so that Christ's power may rest on me. That is why, for Christ's sake, I delight in weaknesses, in insults, in hardships, in persecutions, in difficulties. For when I am weak, then I am strong.

—2 Corinthians 12:7–10 (NIV)

I first met June Masters Bacher at the Christian Booksellers Convention in 1987. I recognized her from the pictures on her books and went over immediately to say hello. She was my number-one competition at Harvest House Publishers, number-one by a long shot. We became instant friends, because that's just the way June is.

June writes Prairie Romances, and her titles always take the top in sales. That year, 1987, Bob Hawkins, Sr., of Harvest House awarded her with a leatherbound volume of a book that had just sold its millionth copy. I was impressed, particularly in light of what June had just told me.

June lives in chronic pain that is so debilitating she must lay flat on her back, getting up only fifteen minutes at a time to write. Most of us would quit, turn on the soap operas by remote control, and feel sorry for ourselves. Not June.

"I prayed for healing," she told me, bolstered for the rough and tumble and autograph parties of CBA with pain-killing drugs, "a release from the iron claws of this pain. But that has failed to come—maybe sometime, but he has healed me in other ways. He gives me the strength to carry on and has blessed me with success, a miracle under the circumstances."

Strength to carry on. Giving and sharing and encouraging, June carries on, not from a position of weakness at all, but from one of incredible strength. I latched onto her, I think, because she provides a role model I need in my own life.

When I had to start going in for painful tests without anesthetic, I wrote to June, confident she'd been through it and could help. She could, and did. "We must be good girls," she told me, "and do all that the doctors tell us. The Lord is with us." And then she added, "And maybe with them!" Now when knives and needles cut in without mercy I remember her joke, and smile.

Last January she wrote another letter typical of God's sustaining strength amidst trying weakness. "By the way," she wrote, "I took a terrible tumble and really did myself in." She'd completely skinned the left side of her face, so badly that grafting had very nearly been required; damaged her not-so-good spine so that it felt broken in about seven places; and sprained, dreadfully, her left wrist. "With arthritis in my right thumb," she wrote, "how to write? Would you believe that very day I completed my next book?"

I believed it.

The beat goes on, as she says, and there is no point in wearying everyone with aches and pains. "We must," she says, "contribute to a world that hurts in other ways. Although," she adds, "I feel I do so little to brighten this world. Perhaps out there somewhere someone has been helped?"

Perhaps? Does she need to ask?

The world is always helped when we give and share and encourage from a position of strength, particularly when it's strength born of God in the midst of weakness. There is always a brightened corner—when the choice to give and share and encourage is ours.

CHRISTY

"Whoever finds his life will lose it, and whoever loses his life for my sake will find it."

—Matthew 10:39 (NIV)

In *Christy,* Miss Henderson, the Quaker missionary, asks nineteen-year-old Christy Huddleston why she has come to the mission in the back hills of Tennessee. Has she, perhaps, gotten carried away with Dr. Ferrand's emotional appeal?

Christy admits that most girls her age can easily be carried away by emotional appeal. But she's had four months to back out and hasn't. She wants, she explains, to teach school, to make her life count, to work with children, but it all sounds so lame when she says it. Why *is* she here? *To find meaning, significance to life?*

Christy Huddleston threw herself into the tasks at hand, sacrificing both energy and time—and her finer "sensibilities." Daily she pushed her nose into perfumed handkerchiefs so she could teach dirty children their sums. Daily she listened to the endless prattle of Ruby Mae. Daily she visited the sick, encouraged the discouraged. Daily she brought pleasure and delight to as many as she could find. But what did it all mean? Why was she doing all this? Dr. MacNeil scorned her inability to name it.

"What does it mean to you?" he wanted to know, when she could only talk of Miss Henderson's beliefs. What was, the doctor insisted, her own working philosophy of life? The more she tried to explain, the more muddled she got and finally, exasperated more with herself than with him, she exploded in fury and ran from the room.

But she carried on. Before long she was called upon to wash and dress a dead baby, killed by a loving, yet superstitious mother. Within weeks she had to confront a man who'd just as soon shoot her dead for yanking his insolent son up by the hair. In the full bloom of spring she wept over the death of her friend, Fairchild, taken by the "Shadow." Giving, and more giving. And then the typhoid epidemic hit and David, the young minister at the mission, urged her to leave.

What? Run away? Think of nothing or no one but her own skin? Why, she couldn't leave! She loved being here! What would she do without Opal's faith? Little Burl Allen's love? Zady's hope? And suddenly she knew why she was here and what life meant.

"You see, David," she said, trying to explain, "it's just that when I volunteered to come to the mountains, I thought it was from really lofty motives—because I loved people and wanted to help them. But now I know that wasn't the reason at all. I came for me."[24]

Jesus said that whoever finds their life will lose it, but that whoever loses their life will find it. And as Christy Huddleston, in the backwoods country of the Tennessee, discovered, we do find meaning and significance when we give, not for someone else, but ourselves—when the choice to give is ours.

MOTHER MARY

"Do not be afraid, Mary, you have found favor with God. You will be with child and give birth to a son, and you are to give him the name Jesus. He will be great and will be called the Son of the Most High. The Lord God will give him the throne of his father David, and he will reign over the house of Jacob forever; his kingdom will never end."

"How will this be," Mary asked the angel, "since I am a virgin?"

—Luke 1:30–34 (NIV)

Was Mary drawing water at the well in Nazareth when the stranger approached? Or was she washing butter, packing it into earthen vessels? What was she doing when a man she'd never seen before said, "Greetings, you who are highly favored! The Lord is with you"?

"Excuse me?"

I wonder, did the bucket fall from her hand, warm water splash across her hot and dusty feet? Did she drop her bowl? Did it break? Did she hasten to gather the precious butter coated now in dust and dirt? Kneeling, scooping, heart beating fast?

Artists for hundreds of years have attempted to draw the expression on Mary's face when told the news of her virgin pregnancy, a face sweet with angelic repose and acceptance. Yet the Bible tells us Mary was troubled. Her eyes must have darted, her fingers trembled. Her mind must have been a tumbler of thoughts and it must have been with great effort that she gathered her wits. "Excuse me, sir," she must have politely said. "But there is work I must do."

"Do not be afraid, Mary."

He knew her name!

Did her heart slow? Did she take a second look? Did she see the angel before her or only a man?

"You have found favor with God," the stranger told her. "You will be with child and give birth to a son, and you are to give him the name Jesus. He will be great and will be called the Son of the Most High."

Child? Her hand involuntarily went to her abdomen. *The Messiah? Does he talk of the Messiah?*

"The Lord God will give him the throne of his father David, and he will reign over the house of Jacob forever; his kingdom will never end."

"But how will this be?" She blushed suddenly at the sound of her own voice and put her hands to her face. "Since I am a virgin?"

"The Holy Spirit will come upon you, and the power of the Most High will overshadow you. So the holy one to be born will be called the Son of God."

But this is impossible! But, she wondered, *what of Elizabeth?*

"Even Elizabeth your relative is going to have a child in her old age." *Did the man read her mind?* "She who is said to be barren is in her sixth month. Nothing is impossible with God."

The thoughts tumbled in Mary's mind as she picked up her bucket or bowl and busied herself, drawing new water, resetting the butter. A child? Me? Elizabeth? But how? Who? Not the Messiah—surely the man jests! *But was he a man?* He stood as if waiting for a response.

No, I don't think Mary's face was one of sweet repose and calm acceptance. There could only have been fright. She had to have thought of Joseph, her betrothed. What would *he* say? He would divorce her. She could even be stoned. Did she gasp? Put a hand to her throat? Her father, her own father! What would he think? *But how could this be?* It can't!

If it was water she'd drawn, did the man walk alongside her down the narrow streets toward her mother's home, carelessly bumping into children who darted too fast before them? If it was butter she'd been washing, did he take the pat from her hand and find a new bowl? Did he help pick up the broken shards?

How long did it take Mary to make her choice, a choice to martyr herself to the will of God, *for surely this man must be an angel?* How long did it take before she turned, eyes still troubled with things she couldn't understand, but mind made up, to say to the stranger—angel, "I am the Lord's servant."

We have no way of knowing. But we do know it was her choice. She willingly sacrificed her reputation, her marriage, her very life to something she could not fully comprehend. "May it be to me as you have said," she said, giving the angel her assent.

It wasn't until Elizabeth, six months pregnant, confirmed the truth of the stranger's words that Mary's fear vanished and the peace of the artist's pictures found its place in her heart. Only when Elizabeth said, "Blessed are you among women," did Mary lose her troubled thoughts. Listen! Can you hear her joy when she sings?

> My soul glorifies the Lord
> and my spirit rejoices in God my Savior,
> for he has been mindful
> of the humble state of his servant.
> From now on all generations will call me blessed,
> for the Mighty One has done great things for me—
> holy is his name.

The artist says there is sweet repose and calm acceptance when martyrdom is thrust into our laps, but this is not so. For a time we may be troubled, as was Mary, but in the end, as we begin to understand, we will find peace, as did Mary, when the choice for martyrdom is ours.

$\mathscr{L}$OVING OURSELVES
The Forgotten Commandment

". . . love your neighbor as yourself. I am the Lord."
—Leviticus 19:18 (NIV)

"Teacher, which is the greatest commandment in the Law?"
Jesus replied: " 'Love the Lord your God with all your heart and
with all your soul and with all your mind.' This is the first
and greatest commandment. And the second is like it: 'Love
your neighbor as yourself.' All the Law and the Prophets hang
on these two commandments."
—Matthew 22:36–40 (NIV)

"We were just wondering," Dorothy has asked the Tinman, "if you couldn't come with us to the Emerald City to ask the Wizard of Oz for a heart." But oddly enough, the Tinman, remember, responded far differently than one might have expected. "Well . . . " he'd said, voice full of doubt, "suppose the Wizard wouldn't give me one when we got there?"

The Tinman's response is significant because he is very much like many of us in the church today. We are women full of self-doubt and who feel unworthy of love, and if we are to believe James and Phyllis Alsdurf, authors of *Battered Into Submission*, there are, conservatively speaking, 22 percent of us in this boat; women, who, like the Tinman, find it hard to believe (for we've been told in so many subtle and not so subtle ways) that what we need is not ours—just for the asking and because we deserve it.[25] Sad to say, approximately one out of every four of us sitting in the pews every Sunday morning feels this way. And so we resort to "singing for our supper" in hopes of getting what we need.

We wash and cook and stand in grocery lines and go to meetings and pick up the dry cleaning and teach our Sunday school classes and blow dry our hair and run two miles and go on a diet and, and, and . . . all in the hopes we will be rewarded and given a measure of consideration. Unlike the king who counts out his money while his maid hangs up his clothes, and unlike Old King Cole who can just call for his pipe and call for his bowl, we scurry about, jockeying for what we need.

I'll scratch your back. I'll turn the other cheek. I'll go the second mile. I'll even give the coat off my back. We give and give and give, and give again, until suddenly we're no longer giving of ourselves anymore, but bargaining for the security and love that ought to be ours in the first place. Our martyrdom dissolves into nothing more than manipulation, to ensure our own needs—not someone else's. We are not Martyrs at all, we are pseudo-Martyrs.

The tragic part is that we don't actively *know* we're unloved; but we do suspect it. Which is why all the busy behavior. We pseudo-martyr ourselves away, desperate to keep from facing the bitter truth. *Are we loved?*

One way to tell is to quit performing, to quit giving and sacrificing, and see what happens. It sounds threatening, doesn't it? But my husband . . . But my boss . . . But my daughter, but my church, but the ladies' group, but, but, but . . . Why are we afraid to stop? Why? Why are *you* afraid? Do you, like I once did, feel unloved? And is this why you give so much? Eeyore in *Winnie-The-Pooh* felt unloved when everyone forgot his birthday, and who wouldn't? So he did what we all do. He manipulated the conversation around to his birthday—to see if he could get the assurance he needed that Pooh and Piglet cared. When they at last dutifully asked why he was so sad, he said he wasn't. It was his birthday, after all, the happiest day of the year.

Whenever we feel unloved we wind up like Eeyore, the pseudo-Martyr, and instead of generating redemption, which is what being a true Martyr is all about, we generate guilt. Poor Pooh and poor Piglet, feeling terribly guilty, had to scamper off quick as a wink, Pooh one way, Piglet another, to get poor Eeyore a present at once.

And Eeyore? Needy, feeling unloved, he—and we—are not in a very good position to offer genuine sacrifice, are we? We are too concerned about our own unmet needs, and it's not that this is right or wrong (for our needs must be met), it is our reality.

The answer, though, is not to buckle down and give even more of ourselves, which is what I tried to do for many years—and which I still catch myself doing. I still tend to turn myself inside out, trying to get people to "remember my birthday." But the answer is not to turn ourselves inside out and sad like Eeyore, but to start loving ourselves.

Not an easy task, for a lot of us. In the first place, it flies in the face of all we've been taught. Remember the old J-O-Y slogan from primary days at Sunday school: Jesus first, Others next, Yourself last? J-O-Y? Scott Peck in *The Road Less Traveled* refutes this theory as impossible, though, and we need to listen. "We are incapable," he says, "of loving another unless we love ourselves."[26] Jesus agrees. "Love your neighbor as yourself," he says, but we keep interpreting it to mean *instead of.*

In the second place, if the truth were to be known, loving oneself feels to the pseudo-martyr like cutting off all chance of *being* loved. No one will love me, we think, if I love and take care of myself. Right? I mean, what will happen when I decide to go to school? Take the job? Shoot for the promotion? Spend time on myself? Spend *money* on myself? If I don't sacrifice myself for all those others in my life, no one will even *like* me anymore!

Maybe so. And this may very well be a sacrifice we have to make—sacrificing that need to be loved. I know I had to. As long as we *need* to be loved, we can't *receive* love. "If being loved is your goal," says Peck, banging me and you and Eeyore over the head with the truth, "you will fail to achieve it." He goes on to say, "The only way to be assured of being loved is to be a person worthy of love,"[27] and we're right back to loving ourselves first and attaching to ourselves a measure of worth.

"But!" we say, terrified of birthdays going by unnoticed. But! Look at what happened to Eeyore—not over his birthday, but over something else. Something a little more serious.

Eeyore didn't have a house. He lived in a field. And one winter it got pretty cold, snow flying around, and no one thought to build him a house! They had gray fluff blown into their heads by mistake he told Christopher Robin. But here Eeyore, instead of feeling sorry for himself, took a different tack. He built *himself* a house.

What it comes down to, is that Eeyore decided to risk not manipulating his friends into meeting his needs (like he did at his birthday) and instead accepted the fact that maybe they really didn't care if he froze to death, that maybe he really wasn't loved—and he made the choice to love himself instead. He built his own house even though it felt dreadfully, horribly, incurably selfish to meet his own needs.

Eight years ago it was a little cold in my field too, only I was not nearly so capable as even poor Eeyore. Unloved and feeling as though I might "freeze to death" because no one would take care of me, I was fortunate enough to have a doctor—no gray fluff in his ears—who was quite concerned.

I was having to go in for a series of weekly experimental IV injections and he started giving me the task, each week, of finding something I could do just for myself. Progress was slow. I found it very difficult to put the Y before the O, and J-Y-O kept clanging in my head like warped cymbals. Finally he took to writing prescriptions, sending me not to the pharmacy but to the shopping malls. He eased me into it. First a bottle of nail polish. When I got so I could do that without feeling too terribly selfish, he increased the "dose." Gradually, he taught me to love myself enough to take care of my own needs and a miracle occurred. People started loving me. And poor Eeyore? Once he took it into his head to do something nice for himself—like build a house when he needed one—he found himself loved as well. No sooner had he gotten the job done, and gone to tell Christopher Robin all about it, when Pooh and Piglet, sitting on a gate in the snow, got to thinking about poor Eeyore, about how he had no house of his own, about the snowy, cold field, about how maybe they could build him a house—so they did. A nice little house right at Pooh Corner.

Loving ourselves always invites others to do the same.

And this is the miracle people like you and me and Eeyore are slow to learn. If we value ourselves, other people will value us as well—without being *manipulated* into it. And in the end we receive all the love we could ever ask for, and more.

Now I know this is Pooh Corner and not where we live, and that those who live at *our* house don't always love us back as did Piglet and Pooh. Sometimes they leave us behind; sometimes they even take the house with them. But our fairy tales remind us that love does abound. Cinderella. Rapunzel. Thumbelina. And what about the Bible's very own fairy tale? What about Ruth?

According to Jewish law a kinsman could redeem Ruth, but her closest kinsman-redeemer rejected her. Which is important for those of us who risk not being loved in order to love ourselves. The process often leaves us rejected. But the Bible assures us that if we are committed to loving ourselves as much as, and not instead of, our neighbors, there is a *second* kinsman-redeemer waiting in the wings—there is Boaz. For the truth is, there is no shortage of loving people in this world—not if we love ourselves enough to bring them out of the woods.

I discovered this to be true in my own life, as did Eeyore, as did Ruth, and as did the Tinman in *The Wizard of Oz.*

"Oil my arms please," said the Tinman, "oil my elbows." He loved himself enough to ask that his needs be met and in the process he found that he was loved by both the Scarecrow and Dorothy in return.

Because this is just the way it works. Once we begin to love ourselves, others do respond.

And what this does for me, for you, for Eeyore, the Tinman, and Ruth of the Old Testament and everyone else, is free us up to make choices for *honest* sacrifice based on love and not need, and we move into a whole new realm of giving. No longer pseudo-martyr bargaining for worth and love, full of doubts about ourselves, we are free to make redemptive choices for the good of others— because we've chosen to, with no thought of return.

"Dorothy," says the Tinman, "I'll see you reach the Wizard, whether I get a heart or not."

Such choices for this kind of honest martyrdom put us back on the yellow brick road, though, with the wicked witch and her fireballs. Many of us resist. It's so much easier to remain the pseudo-Martyr, frittering away our lives with piecemeal and sometimes very painful sacrifices—because it excuses us from the bigger issues, like getting Dorothy to the Wizard in the Emerald City. A battered woman doesn't have to resolve evil on a grand scale if she's consumed on a personal level. A busy housewife doesn't have to reach out and help anyone else if she's consumed with her own "sacrificial" affairs. A college professor doesn't have to help a struggling student if she's consumed by academic politics that bleed her of energy and time. If we can feel sanctimonious about the martyrdom we experience in our own backyard, strung up on a pole of everyone else's expectations or rusting away uselessly in the woods, we never have to do anything redemptive in the wicked world beyond the picket gate and down the road. When we can whine about self-imposed pain, we need not ever risk real pain.

But the courageous rally forth, for like the Tinman we want a heart. We want to know how to sacrifice redemptively and to give of ourselves for the good of others.

It's a little scary. "I don't like this forest," says Dorothy when the three newfound friends round a bend in the yellow brick road, "it's dark and creepy." The Tinman, the Scarecrow, and Dorothy, all three pause, arm in arm, and look about apprehensively, sensing dragons that could inflict real pain. The sun is gone. The air is damp. The music has suddenly grown menacing and we shiver, hearing now the frightening forest noises. "Do you suppose we'll meet any wild animals?" Dorothy asks.

"Um, some," says the Tinman. "But mostly lions, tigers, and bears."

"Lions and tigers and bears, oh my." They hasten forward. "Lions and tigers and bears, oh my! *Lions and tigers and bears, oh my!*" Arm in arm, faster and faster they hurry through the woods. *"Lions and tigers and bears, oh my! LIONS AND TIGERS AND BEARS, OH MY!"* Faster and faster. They break into a run. *"LIONS AND TIGERS AND BEARS, OH MY!"*

During World War II Corrie ten Boom, despite her faith in God, found it terribly frightening to be a Martyr and face the unknown of lions and tigers and bears—until she remembered the words of her martyred father, a wise and loving man.

"Corrie," he'd said gently when she was only a little girl, "when you and I go to Amsterdam—when do I give you your ticket?"

"Just before we get on the train."

"Exactly. And our wise Father in heaven knows when we're going to need things too. Don't run ahead of him, Corrie. When the time comes . . . you will look into your heart and find the strength you need—just in time."[28]

"ROAR-RR"! A lion leaps from the forest. The Scarecrow and the Tinman fall back. Dorothy flies behind a tree. The Lion makes a jab at the Tinman, the Scarecrow! They cower in defeat!

Toto barks!

"I'll get *you* anyway, Pee-wee!" the Lion roars, taking off after Dorothy's little dog. But wait—Dorothy springs into action.

"Corrie, when you and I go to Amsterdam—when do I give you your ticket?"

"Just before we get on the train."

"When the time comes . . . you will look into your heart and find the strength you need."

In order to protect her dog, Dorothy flies out from behind her tree and grabs Toto into her arms—strength and courage hers, just in time. She is ready to die to save the little dog she loves. And this is what the role of Martyr is all about: knowing and thinking and loving—enough to sacrifice for the redemption of those we love.

But wait— Dorothy strikes back. She slaps the Lion across the nose. *"Shame on you!"* she says, stunning us all. She has changed her mind. She is not going to martyr herself after all. She is going to fight back. She is going to be a Warrior—for while there are dragons that can be redeemed, there also some dragons that *can,* and must, be slain. And we are ready for the next task of the journey: learning what it means to be a Warrior, and to fight.

NOTES

1. Dialogue from Walt Disney video *Cinderella.*

2. Matthew 14:14 (TEV).

3. Matthew 12:15 (TEV).

4. Mark 8:4 (TEV).

5. John 6:15 (TEV).

6. Luke 18:15–17 (TEV).

7. Matthew 12:39 (TEV).

8. John 10:17, 18 (RSV). [emphasis mine]

9. Carol Pearson, *The Hero Within* (San Francisco, Harper & Row, 1986), 105.

10. Pearson, *The Hero Within,* 106.

11. Mark 8:35 (RSV).

12. Rufus Jones, *The Quakers in the American Colonies* (New York: W. W. Norton Co., Inc., 1966), 70, 71.

13. *Records of Massachusetts Colony,* vol. iv. part i., 345.

14. *Records of Massachusetts Colony,* 383.

15. Jones, *The Quakers in the American Colonies,* 85.

16. *Records of Massachusetts Colony,* 384.

17. *Records of Massachusetts Colony,* 419.

18. Joshua 2:12 (NIV).

19. Joshua 6:17 (KJV).

20. Johanna Johnston, *Runaway to Heaven* (Garden City, NY: Double-day, 1963), 199.

21. Charlotte Bronte, *Jane Eyre* (New York: New American Library, 1960).

22. Lenore Weitzman, *The Divorce Revolution* (New York: The Free Press, 1987), 325.

23. Brenda Wilbee, "Part of the Family," *Moody Monthly,* October 1987, 20.

24. Catherine Marshall, *Christy* (New York: McGraw-Hill, 1967), 470.

25. James and Phyllis Alsdurf, *Battered Into Submission,* quoted in "Battered Into Submission," *Christianity Today,* 16 June 1989, 24.

26. M. Scott Peck, *The Road Less Traveled* (New York: Simon & Schuster, 1978), 82.

27. Peck, *The Road Less Traveled,* 102.

28. Corrie ten Boom, with John and Elizabeth Sherrill, *The Hiding Place* (Old Tappan, NJ: Chosen Books, 1971).

SIX *Warrior*

"How do I slay this dragon?"

—*Deborah the Warrior*

$\mathcal{A}$ TIME FOR WAR
Even for Women

> *These are the nations the Lord left to test all those Israelites who had not experienced any of the wars in Canaan (he did this only to teach warfare to the descendants of the Israelites who had not had previous battle experience) . . .*
>
> *Deborah, a prophetess, the wife of Lappidoth, was leading Israel at that time.*
>
> —Judges 3:1, 2; 4:4 (NIV)

Sometimes we have to fight back. The Orphan, Pilgrim, or Martyr options don't always solve the problem. In *The Wizard of Oz* poor Dorothy had about all she could take. First Miss Gulch, then the wicked Witch of the West, and now a roaring Lion. "Shame on you!" she hollered, moving swiftly and forcefully into the Warrior role, smacking the Lion a good one. "It's bad enough when you pick on a straw man, but when you go around picking on poor little dogs!"

When the church teaches women and children to always turn the other cheek, they do everyone great disservice—for some dragons simply do not respond to anything but brute force. Scott Peck says, "I have learned nothing in twenty years that would suggest that evil people can be rapidly influenced by any means other than raw power. They do not respond, at least in the short run, to either gentle kindness or any form of spiritual persuasion . . . "[1] Sometimes, the Warrior learns, it takes a slap across the nose to save Toto.

The Canaanites thirteen centuries before Christ apparently needed a slap too. For twenty years they'd been oppressing the Israelites, and the Israelites, like Dorothy, were about fed up. But they, unlike Dorothy, were afraid. Sisera, commander of the

Canaanite army, had nine hundred iron chariots. Everyone, men and women alike, cowered in the face of such overwhelming odds. Everyone, that is, but Deborah.

Deborah is one of the more fascinating women of the Bible. Wife of Lappidoth, an obscure man in Hebrew history, she was the only woman to rise to the height of political power by consent of the people. She was judge, ruler, prophet, and military hero, and few women in world history have attained such public respect, supreme authority, and military command.

She held court under the royal Palm of Deborah, on the open road between Ramah and Bethel in the hill country of Ephraim, where Samuel would some day be born. There she heard cases of controversy and dispensed justice, and it was there she heard the increasingly frequent stories of oppression from the Canaanites. She burned with indignation. Why was this being allowed to continue? She called to her court Barak, one of the country's most capable military men. "The Lord God," she told him in no uncertain terms, "has commanded that you take ten thousand men from Naphtali and Zebulun and lead the way to Mount Tabor. I myself will go down and lure Sisera, the commander of Jabin's army, with all his chariots and troops, to the Kishon River so you can storm them by force."

"If you go with me, I'll go," the military captain said. "But if you don't, I won't."

We learn from Josephus (and indirectly from the Song of Deborah in Judges 5) that when Deborah and Barak led their troops against Sisera a storm came up. Sleet and hail burst over the valley from the east and drove straight into the face of Sisera and his army.[2] "Up!" cried Deborah from where she and Barak stood on a lofty rock watching the slingers and archers below disabled by the biting cold. "For this is the day in which the Lord hath delivered Sisera into thine hand! See? Is not the Lord gone out before thee?"

Rain and wind to their backs, down they swept, ten thousand and a woman, against nine hundred iron chariots stuck in the mud of the raging Kishon River. Not a man was spared.

Sometimes God calls women to war. When the dragon roars, nine hundred chariots downwind, we wind up on the front line whether we like it or not. Deborah. You. Me.

We resist, however. Being a Warrior is a man's role, and we know that for us to take up arms is to strike at the very heart of what it means to be a woman. Female Warriors have always been punished, silenced swiftly by such labels as "sexual deviant" or "insane." Anne Hutchinson, when she taught that women could interpret the word of God just as capably as men, was declared by Puritan Boston to be a "rebel with a confused, bewildered mind, and a woman 'whose stern and masculine mind . . . triumphed over the tender affections of a wife and mother.' "[3] She was banished. Leaders of the suffrage movement were called lesbians and dismissed. Harriet Beecher Stowe was considered a busybody who didn't take care of her family. Today feminists who want nothing more than equal rights are called man haters. The voice of argument, if delivered by a woman, is often neither here nor there. A woman Warrior is unacceptable in our culture, and we need only look at Walt Disney's *Dumbo* to see the truth of this.

The stork delivers a baby to Mrs. Jumbo, who is "expecting," and all the old ladies hang their trunks over the partition to see. My, my, what a cutey he is. Kootchy-kootchy-coo. One leans over to tickle his chin.

"Katchoo!" Out flop two very big ears.

There is a horrified gasp. Suddenly the exclamations turn caustic. "Look at those E-A-R-S," whispers one, loud enough of course so Mrs. Jumbo is sure to hear.[4]

"What? Ears! Oh, yes! Aren't they funny?" Titter, titter.

The elephant who'd just finished tickling the baby's chin now reaches down to pull on the ears. Mrs. Jumbo smacks the offending trunk. WHOMP! Just like Dorothy with the Lion.

"What a temper!" says one of the old biddies.

"It was a perfectly harmless remark," says another.

"Who cares about her precious Little Jumbo?" says a third.

"Jumbo?" laughs a fourth. "You mean *Dumbo!*" Ripples of laughter erupt.

Furious, Mrs. Jumbo sees the peg that holds the partition door up, and up swings her trunk. BANG! Down swings the door and Dumbo is spared any more cruelty.

But later, when the circus is in full swing, a little boy with big ears comes by and starts to tease poor Dumbo. "Isn't that the funniest thing you ever saw?" he jeers, sticking out his tongue and waggling it before ducking under the fence to blow in Dumbo's ear. Mrs. Jumbo the Warrior picks up the insolent little boy with her trunk, drapes him over the chain fence, and proceeds to

soundly spank his upturned bottom, a perfectly understandable—
and appropriate—response to the conflict at hand.

But this is unacceptable. A female Warrior? Everyone comes
running; circus hands generate panic where no panic need be,
throwing lassos and frightening poor Jumbo into a bellowing, de-
fensive fight. Up she goes on her hind legs, trumpeting. The ropes
slide over her neck, yank tight. Down she comes. Her punishment
is swift and sure. She is separated from the baby she loves, led
away to solitary confinement with bars on the windows. A bold
sign is banged into place: DANGER! MAD ELEPHANT! Even in Walt
Disney, a woman Warrior is declared insane.

No wonder we fear the Warrior role above all others. We'd
rather do *anything* than look a dragon in the eye and say, "You are
a dragon and I am going to slay you." The dragon breathes fire, real
fire. We're going to get burned and burned badly. There is going
to be blood, most likely ours, and someone is going to get upset.
Few of us have courage enough to face such horror. We're not
Dorothy at all, or even Jumbo. Rather, we're the cowardly Lion and
we don't mind admitting it.

"You're right, I am a coward," the Lion confesses to Dorothy. "I
haven't any courage at all."

The immediate task of the Warrior, then, is to come to terms
with personal fear—just as the cowardly Lion had to do. We do
this, says Julie Andrews in *The Sound of Music,* by "facing it."
Which is what the Wizard (in his bumbling way) understood.
When Dorothy, the Scarecrow, and the Tinman finally get in to see
him, he says, "You must prove yourselves worthy by performing a
very small task. Bring me the broomstick of the wicked Witch of
the West." Not even God can hand out homes, brains, hearts, and
courage. We have to prove these things ourselves.

Not easy to bring in the broomstick. "But what if she kills us
first?" the cowardly Lion, trembling, asks.

"I said GO!"

The Lion flees, and so do we.

When Meredith was first separated from her husband, her six-
year-old daughter was attending first grade at a local parochial
school. There were only six weeks left in the year and Meredith
had no money to pay the tuition. It pained her to think of trans-
ferring her daughter to public school for such a short time, par-

ticularly since she'd be required to ride a bus three-quarters of an hour one way. Life was disruptive enough. Yet her father refused to lend a hand, and for Meredith to keep Cary at Holy Trinity of God was like the Lion being asked to get the witch's broomstick. Emotionally, she fled.

Pearson in *The Hero Within* says that because women are so afraid of the Warrior role, they are often only "seduced" into the fray to save others.[5] Only when our back is up against the wall do we come out flying, never mind our fear. Deborah the prophet. Jumbo the elephant. Dorothy the Orphan. You. Me. Meredith.

Even the cowardly Lion.

When the wicked witch captures Dorothy, the three friends wind their way up a craggy mountain to the witch's lair to rescue Dorothy. "I've got a plan," says the Scarecrow when they stop for a rest and consultation, "on how to get in there. And you," he says, looking at the Lion, "are going to lead us."

"I gotta get her out of there?" the Lion asks, trembling, holding his tail. We all tremble. Impossible. Dangerous. *"I have to keep Cary in school?"* Suddenly the Lion says, surprising us all, "All right. I'll go in there. For Dorothy."

Meredith too, trembling, holding her tail, had to say, "All right. I'll do it. For Cary."

Love and *the need to protect* do seduce us into the fray—and like the cowboy who gets back up on the horse that threw him, it's the battle that teaches us how very courageous we really are.

Meredith knew her husband had a savings account in a bank in California somewhere. But where? Which bank? And how much? She started to call around, praying for the Lion's "nerve" each time she dialed. It may seem an easy task to us, but for Meredith, a woman who'd never been allowed access to money, this was terrifying. She had no idea what she was doing. Too, she'd never ever gone behind her husband's back and done anything without approval. This frightened her more than asking, "Do you have an account for Mr. and Mrs. . . . " Finally someone said yes.

The account had three thousand dollars in it. She breathed a sigh of relief. But wait, eighteen hundred of it had been drawn out in the last month. "Eighteen hundred?" she shrieked. Cary's first grade picture hung off the wall, and, front teeth missing, she smiled down at Meredith. "How," Meredith asked, finding a Lion's nerve, "do I get the rest out?"

"Two hundred of the remaining twelve hundred," the man went on to explain, "isn't mature yet. But if you send me a letter asking for the thousand I can send you a check."

Meredith wrote the letter, still trembling. So sneaky. She put it out for the postman. So mean. By night she was in a state. She called her husband.

"I just wanted you to know," she said, "that I withdrew a thousand dollars from the savings account in California. But I needed that money," she hastened to explain, "to keep Cary in school. You wouldn't—"

"When did you close it out?"

"You can have the other two hundred. I—"

"When'd you send the letter?"

"Today. They told me—"

He laughed. "Oh, that's too bad. I sent in a withdrawal slip three days ago closing out the account."

The Tinman, the Scarecrow, and the Lion are all making plans when three guards come over the wall and jump them. So much for the best laid plans of mice and men. Meredith hung up. Heat in her gut. She stumbled for the couch. The dragon laughed in her face and she rocked herself back and forth, unbelieving. How could a father deny his daughter what he could afford to give? More to the point, *how* she wondered, seeing only the impossible fortress of poverty, *was she going to keep Cary in school?*

She knew she was being called to the front lines and was scared. In Judges 3 the Lord left the remnants of four nations in the Promised Land—to test the Israelites who had not yet experienced war. This was Meredith. This is me. This is you. This is *any* of us who've never learned we sometimes have to fight in order to bring about change for good in a fallen world. But how, if the guards have all come over the wall and jumped us? How, if the dragon strikes back?

Sometimes courage isn't enough.

But God is. Weren't we all surprised when the Scarecrow, the Tinman, and the Lion peered over the rocky ridge wearing the enemy's clothes? But Deborah, was she so surprised when wind and sleet drove down from heaven to swell the Kishon River and mire the wheels of her enemy's chariots? The very next night after the dragon laughed in Meredith's face she got a phone call. "How much did you say you withdrew?" her husband wanted to know.

"A thousand."

"I filled out my withdrawal slip for the whole twelve hundred," he told her, "only two hundred isn't mature." Meredith knew that. What was he getting at? "My slip," said her husband "for twelve hundred bounced." Her heart lurched into double time.

"You mean I get the money?"

"No. I'll be over Friday to pick it up."

Friday night his eyes bored into hers. "Give me the check."

She wavered. Then remembering her daughter upstairs in bed, she looked him straight in the eye. "No."

As soon as she heard the front door close, she went upstairs. Moonlight fell through the open curtain onto her little girl's face. "I was glad," Meredith told me, "that she couldn't see me lay the broomstick at her feet."

Yes, sometimes God calls us to war. As women we're afraid of it, we're not very good at it, and a lot of times we are crushed by the backswing. But God, we find, is there in the thick of it.

Dorothy said, "Shame on you!"

The cowardly Lion said, "Wicked witch or no wicked witch, gods or no gods, I'll tear 'em apart. I may not come out alive, but I'm going in there."

This is what we are sometimes called to do. But unlike the Lion, we know there is a God. He doesn't hand out homes, brains, hearts, or courage. He leads us instead straight into battle so we might find the courage we seek and prove to ourselves and our world that if we but dare to fight, some dragons can be slain.

BRENDA

There is a time for everything,
and a season for every activity under heaven . . .
A time for war and a time for peace.

—*Ecclesiastes 3:1, 8b* (NIV)

Several years ago I had an appointment with an optometrist. The contacts I had been wearing for fifteen years had suddenly started to blur and I was blinking a lot. Things did not start off well when I was kept waiting for an hour and a half and only deteriorated when, after five minutes of throwing a few numbers on the wall and trying a few lenses in front of my eyes, he left for a fifteen-minute coffee break. "Where'd you get the donuts today?" I heard him ask someone in a back room. Meanwhile, I sat drumming my fingers on the arm of a chair that held me three feet off the floor. But because I was still in the mode where one must always be pleasant, I was smiling when he came back in.

Without any further examination, he sat down and spat out a diagnosis that made no sense and sent me on my way—still smiling and even exchanging pleasantries. After all, one must be pleasant at all times. When I got the bill for seventy-five dollars, though, I quit smiling and quit being pleasant.

I sent the man a check for twenty-five dollars and told him it was all he was going to get. I explained that I'd gone to an oph-thalmologist since seeing him and was given a full examination. I was diagnosed as having an allergy to the spring pollens and given eye drops that resolved the problem within days. The bill for that was only fifty-four dollars. There simply was no way, I wrote, I could justify paying a higher fee to a mere optometrist who apparently did not know what he was doing.

This was one of the first times I poked a sleeping dragon. Fire erupted. The enraged optometrist sent the check back with a stern warning he would turn me over to a collection agency if I did not pay up. He stamped DELINQUENT ACCOUNT across a statement he'd made up special for the occasion. To be honest, such power scared me. I had to either pay or suffer a black mark on a credit rating I'd worked so hard to keep clean. Kill or be killed, and there wasn't a whole lot I could do with this highway robbery. For days

I went around in my own rage. Who was he to make up what amounted to a phony bill and have all the blessings of a system that would come down hard on me? Then it dawned on me while stirring the chili one night—if he could turn me over to a collection agency, why couldn't I do the same to him?

Taking a deep breath, for the idea of choices was still new to me, I sent him back the twenty-five dollar check—along with a bill for fifty to cover the time I'd spent waiting in his office. "You have thirty days to pay," I wrote, "or I'll turn you over to a collection agency. It would, however, be much easier if you would just accept the twenty-five dollars as payment in full. This would effectively cancel our mutual debts to each other."

I never heard from him again, but I did get my canceled check for twenty-five dollars back, with his signature acknowledging payment in full. It goes to show, when we dare to fight, we find that some dragons can be slain.

JAEL

All the troops of Sisera fell by the sword; not a man was left. Sisera, however, fled on foot to the tent of Jael, the wife of Heber the Kenite, because there were friendly relations between Jabin king of Hazor and the clan of Heber the Kenite.

Jael went out to meet Sisera and said to him, "Come, my lord, come right in. Don't be afraid." So he entered her tent, and she put a covering over him.

"I'm thirsty," he said. "Please give me some water." She opened a skin of milk, gave him a drink, and covered him up.

"Stand in the doorway of the tent," he told her. "If someone comes by and asks you, 'Is anyone here?' say 'No.'"

But Jael, Heber's wife, picked up a tent peg and a hammer and went quietly to him while he lay fast asleep, exhausted. She drove the peg through his temple into the ground, and he died.

—Judges 4:16b–21 (NIV)

When Deborah and Barak plunged down the hill to meet the mired chariots of Sisera, not a man was spared. But it took a second woman to complete the battle. Sisera, abandoning his chariot, had raced wind and sleet for safety.

Winded, exhausted, a man on the run, he came to the tent of Jael, wife of Heber the Kenite, a man at peace with the Canaanites. Here Sisera thought he'd be safe. "I'm thirsty," he said. "May I have some water?" Jael opened a skin of milk and invited him to rest.

Weary and worn and miserably cold, he curled up in front of the fire, commanding her to stand guard at the tent's door. "If anyone comes by, tell them no one is here!" Only moments passed and he was asleep.

What would you do? Jael did not like Sisera any better than Deborah liked him. I wonder if she, although married to a Kenite, was Hebrew. Why else would she pick up a hammer and pry loose a tent peg, her only weapon, and set the point to Sisera's temple? Had her sister's children been plundered by the Canaanites? Had her mother been made a widow? Had her place of worship been desecrated? Her God mocked?

How long did she hesitate, debating the Warrior within? Did she whisper a prayer for courage when she pulled back the hammer and sent the peg crashing through bone and brain, pinning him to the ground? I don't know, but the Bible tells us that when Barak arrived in hot pursuit, she ran to greet him. "Come," she said, drawing him into her home, "and I will show you the man you seek."

Sisera was dead, victory won. "Blessed above women," sang Deborah, "shall Jael the wife of Heber the Kenite be." Blessed, for when we dare to fight, even with just a tent peg, we find that dragons can be slain.

DOROTHY

You will keep in perfect peace him whose mind is steadfast,
because he trusts in you.

—*Isaiah 26:3* (KJV)

"Kent?" A glance, and Dorothy King's eyes took it all in. Hospital bed, traction, the sling, respirator, and behind the tubes and IVs her son's head and face so swollen she couldn't recognize him. *Another accident.*

Dorothy King was no stranger to accidents. Mother of five sons, she'd long before accepted the calamities that accompany five healthy boys growing up on a farm. Eleven broken bones between them, two emergency surgeries, another two surgeries to splice tricky breaks, a car wreck, a motorcycle wreck, numerous minibike wrecks. After a while she quit counting.

Then came a phone call in 1978 from Calgary, Alberta, Canada, eclipsing them all. Her second son, just turned twenty, had set out from their Pennsylvania dairy farm to cross the country on a motorbike trip with three of his friends, and now a stranger was telling her of an accident just outside Banff. Could they do emergency surgery? "Why?" she asked again. Punctured lungs. Lacerated liver. Crushed ribs. Two broken legs. Intestines so mangled they'd probably never work again. But that wasn't the worst: Mike's back was crushed. If he lived, he'd be paralyzed from the waist down.

Mike did live, and Dorothy King thought the worst was over. But the phone was ringing again, five years later. Another motorcycle wreck. Sarasota, Florida, this time. This time Kent, her fourth son.

The nightmare returned. As in Mike's case, strangers performed all-night emergency surgery while she made frantic arrangements to fly out before it was too late. As with Mike, the prognosis was not good. As with Mike, the injuries were endless. As with Mike, she stood in shock at the end of the bed, hardly able to register the magnitude of the trauma. Severe concussion. Bruised lung. Ruptured spleen. Hole gouged from stomach to bladder. Broken pelvis. Crushed wrist. Snapped ankle. Shattered kneecap. Compound fracture below the knee. Cut jugular. The only reason he was alive was because a bystander had known how to stem the bleeding that would have left him dead in two minutes.

"Kent?" she whispered, slipping quickly around the respirator to squeeze between heart monitor and oxygen tank. *Bleep. Bleep-bleep . . . bleep.* Hiss-swoosh, hiss-swoosh. Erratic heartbeats. Oxygen pushing in, sucking out. She went all weak in the knees when she saw the worst. He was bleeding from his eyes, and in vain she searched for recognition of her nineteen-year-old son. Nothing. "Kent?" A wash of cold. Unlike Mike he did not respond. Oh, how could she go through this again? *Oh, God, how?*

Thou wilt keep him in perfect peace whose mind is stayed on thee, because he trusteth in thee.

Five years earlier, just after Mike's accident, her father had died of cancer. A man of God, he'd always memorized Scripture. After taking him home to die, she used to sit with him for hours. "Will you," she'd asked him one day, "pass on to me, before you go, the blessing of your memory work?" And so as Isaac to Jacob and Jacob to Joseph, her father passed on to her his family legacy, the desire to memorize Scripture. And as she sat watching for any sign of life in her son's face, verses she'd memorized slowly came to her, thawing her cold, frightened mind.

She reached for Kent's hand and curled her trembling fingers into his. Did she trust God? Slowly her trembling stilled; slowly peace warmed her heart. One by one the verses came, staying her mind on God. They were in God's hands, just as they'd always been. The nurse came in. Her five minutes were up. She could come back in an hour.

Today Dorothy King looks at Kent, healthy and well, and remembers that some dragons *can* be slain.[6]

LITTLE RED RIDING HOOD

Saul sent men to David's house to watch it and to kill him in
the morning. But Michal, David's wife, warned him, "If you
don't run for your life tonight, tomorrow you'll be killed. So
Michal let David down through a window, and he fled and
escaped. Then Michal took an idol and laid it on the bed,
covering it with a garment and putting some goats' hair at the
head.

—*1 Samuel 19:11–13* (NIV)

Once upon a time Little Red Riding Hood was more than a match
for the big bad wolf. How so? you might ask, for Little Red Riding
Hood is *not* someone we see as a Warrior—of *any* kind. We can
blame Charles Perrault for this. In 1697 he took an oral story of a
young woman's rite of passage and made it into a moral fabrication,
adding the red cloak, the male wolf, and tragedy to the disobedient. Of his own distorted version, that of the wolf devouring
naughty Little Red Riding Hood, he had this to say:

> Little girls, this seems to say,
> Never stop upon your way.
> Never trust a stranger-friend;
> No one knows how it will end.
> As you're pretty, so be wise;
> Wolves may lurk in every guise.
> Handsome they may be, and kind,
> Gay, or charming—never mind!
> Now, as then, tis simple truth—
>
> Sweetest tongue has sharpest tooth!

One hundred fifteen years later the Grimm brothers added a
happy ending, allowing a huntsman to come along and cut free
from the stomach of the beastly wolf poor Little Red Riding Hood
and her grandmother. Both versions, however, veer far from the
original tale. "There is," says Alan Dundes, a University of California anthropologist, "a whole male fantasy that's been tacked onto
the story. Male writers essentially took a female tale and ruined it.

They've made the heroine a frail little thing who has to be rescued."[7]

So what is the original fairy tale if not a story to make women
afraid of the woods and wolves and to teach compliant obedience?
It's a story of daring, of a heroine who is shrewd, brave, tough, and
independent—and who fights back, not in frontal attack but by
subterfuge. And who wins.

Once upon a time a woman asked her daughter to take a hot
loaf of bread and a bottle of milk to her granny. Along the way she
met a wolf who wanted to know where she was going; but this
wolf was not the male, sexual figure of our pop psychologists, for
a wolf was always symbolic of the female in medieval European
culture.

"I'm taking," said the Little Girl, "this hot loaf and a bottle of
milk to my granny."

"What path are you taking? The path of needles or the path of
pins?" And here emerges a story symbolic of a young girl under-
going a social ritual connected with sewing communities. She is
moving out of the initial process of piecing cloth together by pin
to the act of sewing cloth together into something functional and
useful.

"Why, the path of needles!" says the Little Girl.

"Then I shall take the path of pins."

We pick up the tale similar now to Perrault's. The wolf has
eaten Granny whole and taken her place in bed.

"Oh, Granny, what big nostrils you have!" says the Little Girl.

"The better to snuff my tobacco with, my child."

"Oh, Granny, what a big mouth you have!"

"The better to eat you, my child!"

But this is not the story of Little Red Riding Hood. This is the
story of the Little Girl. The Little Girl is *not* a helpless victim,
destroyed through her own passivity. The Little Girl says, "Oh,
Granny, I have to go pee!"

"Do it in the bed."

"Oh, no, Granny. I must do it outside."

"All right, but make it quick." The wolf ties a cord to the Little
Girl's foot and lets her out the door, tugging now and then to make
sure she is still there. But again, the Little Girl is not victimized.
She quickly ties the rope on her foot to the plum tree and by the
time the stupid wolf figures out she is gone, she is safely back at

home—with no lectures from her mother. She doesn't need a lecture. She has fought back and won—as all young women need to learn to do.

Yet this is not what we were taught. Any of us. Like me, you were brought up on Perrault/Grimm versions, and you grew up knowing never to stray from the path, to always be obedient, to see the world as belonging to the male, be they vicious or heroic, and to submit to death and hope for rescue. Such a tragedy, for we have inherited fear instead of valor, compliance instead of dominance, submission instead of shrewdness. And we have inherited a deep-seated fear of fighting back, to our tragic end.

Yet our fairy tales—in their original form—teach us that we can, and we must, fight back. As in the tale of the Little Girl—and not in the one of Little Red Riding Hood—some dragons and wolves can, through subterfuge, be slain.

MAHLAH, NOAH, HOGLAH, MILCAH, TIRZAH

The daughters of Zelophehad . . . belonged to the clans of Manasseh son of Joseph. The names of the daughters were Mahlah, Noah, Hoglah, Milcah and Tirzah. They approached the entrance to the Tent of Meeting and stood before Moses, Eleazar the priest, the leaders and the whole assembly, and said, "Our father died in the desert . . . and left no sons. Why should our father's name disappear from his clan because he had no son? Give us property among our father's relatives."

So Moses brought their case before the Lord and the Lord said to him, "What Zelophehad's daughters are saying is right. You must certainly give them property as an inheritance among their father's relatives and turn their father's inheritance over to them."

—Numbers 27:1–7 (NIV)

Until very recently in time women couldn't own property; they *were* property. The first crack in the door—which was only fully opened in *this* country in *this* century—began way back some thirty-five hundred years before. The Israelites were getting ready to move into the Promised Land.

Prior to leaving Egypt there had been a census. New land was to be apportioned according to the findings, and now that they were ready to apportion it some forty years later, the land, because all the original folks had passed on, was being assigned to the heirs. Zelophehad, descendant of Joseph, died without sons. This took him off the list, his family passing into oblivion.

But wait! He had five daughters.

So what?

Aren't they entitled to some land?

No. They're women.

What difference does that make?

None today. But back then it made a big difference. It made no sense to give a woman an inheritance, she *was* the inheritance; this was so much a part of the collective psyche that no one ever thought to question it. Except the five daughters of Zelophehad: Mahlah, Noah, Hoglah, Milcah, and Tirzah.

They went before Moses and the priest to present their case. "Why should the name of our father be done away from among his family, because he hath no son?"

Moses took the dilemma to God. It was a tough problem to resolve. While they wanted to protect the family name, they weren't so sure they wanted to do it at the cost of allowing women to own land.

"The daughters of Zelophehad speak right," said God. "Thou shalt surely give them a possession of an inheritance among their father's brethren; and thou shalt cause the inheritance of their father to pass unto them." A new law was put into effect, and women for the first time since unrecorded days of patriarchy began, albeit under limited circumstances, to own property.

The Zelophehad case has even more significance when we find in the American Bar Association Journal of February 1924, an article by Henry C. Clark quoting the unprecedented case as being an "early declaratory judgment in which the property rights of women . . . are clearly set forth," and to find that jurists still turn to it at times for opinions. It is considered to be the oldest decided case "that is still cited as an authority."[8]

Because five women, Mahlah, Noah, Hoglah, Milcah, and Tirzah, dared to fight for rights no one had considered before in a court of law, we discover that some dragons can be slain.

GLADYS

"You deaf and dumb spirit," he said, "I command you, come out of him and never enter him again."

The spirit shrieked, convulsed him violently and came out . . .

After Jesus had gone indoors, his disciples asked him privately, "Why couldn't we drive it out?"

He replied, "This kind can come out only by prayer [and fasting]."

—Mark 9:25b–29 (NIV)

Thanksgiving 1989 was different from all others for Gladys Steffenson. Her daughter, Valerie, along with seven others, had secluded herself in the St. Paul Cathedral in St. Paul, Minnesota, to pray and fast until the U.S. government indicated a change in its policy of military support for the government of El Salvador. What precipitated the event was the murder of six Jesuit priests and their housekeepers by the government's military police, an act of such violent proportions that Gladys's daughter decided she had to fight back—with or without her mother's approval.

At first Gladys wasn't sure her daughter was doing the right thing. They weren't activists; they didn't protest much of anything. They were just the typical midwestern family with strong moral values and a complacent trust in the government to attend to the more "weighty" issues. However, as time passed, Gladys found her attitude changing.

"As we visited the little group each day in that dark, cold building," she says, "my attitude changed from concern for my daughter to concern for my government and the evil of our policy toward that tiny country."

Gladys Steffenson wasn't the only one who found her attitude changing. The press was sympathetic, and both newspapers and TV brought daily coverage to the Twin Cities. Large groups started to hold rallies outside, and the mayor, congressmen, the governor and the Speaker of the House, Tom Foley, all gave support by phone calls, visits, and speeches. The final Sunday three thousand filled the cathedral in a huge and solemn prayer vigil. "I was amazed," says Gladys, "to see the power of eight people who dared to fast and pray. What once concerned eight, now concerned thousands."

The fast lasted nineteen days. The group finally agreed that while they had not achieved a major victory, they had made an impact on many lives. They disbanded in time for Christmas, to celebrate the hope we have for dragons yet unslain.

"Fasting is an ancient custom," says Gladys, "one that we don't know much about but should probably practice more. None of us will ever be the same again. I would never have imagined the effect this small group could have in influencing people and events. If we have lost some of our complacency, we won't miss it."

Whenever any of us fight, win or lose, we find that some dragons can still be slain.

PRUDENCE

Being confident of this, that he who began a good work in you will carry it on to completion until the day of Christ Jesus.

—*Philippians 1:6 (NIV)*

Prudence Crandall was a gutsy lady. In 1832 she converted a two-story building in the small town of Canterbury, Connecticut, into a boarding school. She was soon running one of New England's finest, most profitable—and reputable—schools. The citizens of Canterbury were only too proud to have her distinguished establishment in their town. That is, until one day she admitted Sarah Harris, a young black girl.

Parents immediately demanded Sarah's withdrawal. If she wasn't dismissed, they would withdraw their own daughters, and for a few days Prudence vacillated. Her conscience eventually won out, and Sarah, overnight, was an only student.

Prudence had to shut down, but she wasn't licked, not by a long shot. She put an ad in Frank Lloyd Garrison's abolitionist paper, *The Liberator,* advertising for the "highest academic caliber of young black ladies." In two months she was back in business, with almost the same number of students, only this time they were all black.

Canterbury declared war. They began by pelting the students with sticks, stones, and obscenities. While the students were taking a first trip into town the front porch was smeared with excrement, chicken heads, and a dead cat. Windows dripped with splattered eggs. The stores followed up by refusing to sell Prudence supplies, the doctor refused to come out when needed, and the newspaper ran editorials attacking her for disrupting the town's cherished tranquility. Still Sarah was not going to be beaten. Black girls, she had decided, had the right to an education, and she was going to give them one.

Abolitionist friends came through, delivering supplies, and when manure was dumped into the school's well, Prudence's father began delivering daily rations of water from his farm two miles away.

Failing to scare her away, the town moved into the courts by pushing through a bill that forbade anyone to teach a "colored person" not a resident of Connecticut. Prudence refused to comply and was arrested and jailed for one night. She posted bond and kept on, keeping the school open while the case dragged on for a year, finally being dismissed by the highest state court on a technicality.

This infuriated the town of Canterbury and it responded with violence. The school was set on fire, but it was extinguished before much damage was done. It was then raided by masked citizens in the middle of the night. With crowbars they smashed their way in, demolishing everything in sight on the ground floor, ransacking the classrooms, and plundering the office. Prudence and the girls huddled in the bedrooms upstairs, praying that God would intervene. He did; the men left without harming the girls.

But Prudence had had enough; she couldn't fight anymore. What had begun as a fight to defend one black girl's right to an education had escalated into a threat of death for twenty others. Prudently, Prudence retired from teaching. She married her Baptist minister friend, a man who'd stuck with her through thick and thin in the small town of Canterbury when no one else would, and moved out of state.

Surprisingly enough, when Prudence Crandall was eighty-three, the state of Connecticut sent a letter of official apology, along with a small pension, proving once again that with perseverance and pluck some dragons can be slain.

WONDER WOMAN

Now listen, you rich people, weep and wail because of the misery that is coming upon you. Your wealth has rotted, and moths have eaten your clothes. Your gold and silver are corroded. Their corrosion will testify against you and eat your flesh like fire. You have hoarded wealth in the last days. Look! The wages you failed to pay the workmen who mowed your fields are crying out against you. The cries of the harvesters have reached the ears of the Lord Almighty. You have lived on earth in luxury and self-indulgence. You have fattened yourselves in the day of slaughter. You have condemned and murdered innocent men, who were not opposing you.

—James 5:1–6 (NIV)

Two years ago when there was a bill before Congress to raise the national minimum wage by forty cents, I had a student at the university who liked to parrot his father. "If you make the rich pay higher wages," Stack insisted, "they won't be able to hire as many workers, and unemployment will increase. So instead of sniveling for more money," he said, summing it all up, "the poor ought to be *grateful* they at least have a job."

Mrs. Priddy, my son's fifth grade teacher, had a different opinion, and she countered this anti-Robin Hood mentality with the weapon of chalk on a blackboard and the fertile minds of her students. She had them work out, as a math assignment, just exactly how much money a person making minimum wage would earn in a year, and then asked them to contrast that sum first to the Washington state poverty level and then to the average income per year per family. This is what Phillip, at age ten, learned: minimum wage will gross a person $8,008 a year; poverty level is $13,950 a year for a family of four;[9] and the average family of four sees an annual income of $28,165.[10] The average family, my son learned, earns more than twice the poverty level while the millions making minimum wage earn only a hair over half. Phillip came home from school that day wondering why there was all the debate over a measly forty-cent raise when, as he said, minimum wage ought to, at the very least, be doubled.

In recent years we have seen a growing gap between the rich and poor.[11] But where is the Warrior, the Robin Hood of the 1990s?

Dr. William Marston, who invented the systolic blood-pressure test used in lie detectors, found as a result of his work that women are more honest than men in business as verified by criminal records, that 90 percent of women are "gaited to be good," and that women, as indicated in intelligence tests, can do more work in a given time—and more accurately—than men.[12] In 1941, when asked by publisher Charlie Gaines to give his ideas on audience reaction to cartoons, Marston said, "Why don't you give the world a woman heroine?"

But, said Gaines, who ever heard of a woman heroine in cartoons? Dr. Marston thought it was about time we did—for women, he said, tend to fight differently than men. They tend, he said, to fight with honesty, goodness, and intelligence. And so under the pseudonym of Charles Moutlon, Dr. Marston wrote a pilot cartoon strip featuring a woman warrior. She battled, "not to control, to have power over, or to 'pound on' as men are prone to do—but to protect, to correct, and to offer mercy to the repentant."[13]

Wonder Woman took the country by storm. And today, fifty years later, we still see *Wonder Woman* comic books down at the local 7-11 selling like hotcakes. Why?

Because our world is hungry for the weapons women can bring to the fray. Women, generally speaking, do not fight to rule over or to destroy or usurp. They tend to fight, if they fight at all, for justice and peace and fairness for all. "Farewell," says Wonder Woman to her enemy, Amazon, letting him go rather than bashing his head as he justly deserves, "I must lead my warriors into ways of peace."[14] A woman warrior, she demands justice, brings peace, and offers to the repentant—and unrepentant sometimes—grace.

Robin Hood was the hero of our fairy tales. Wonder Woman is the heroine of the comic book. But Phillip's fifth grade teacher is Robin Hood and Wonder Woman off the page, fighting in real life the war against poverty and victimization. And you can bet she's scored her point, and scored it well: Phillip will never pay an employee less than a living wage, even if it's legal to do so.

We too can be warriors like Wonder Woman and Mrs. Priddy at Geneva Elementary, because when we fight with honesty, justice, and mercy there are dragons that can, and really ought to be, slain.

ANNE

"If anyone will not welcome you or listen to your words, shake the dust off your feet when you leave that home or town. I tell you the truth, it will be more bearable for Sodom and Gomorrah on the day of judgment than for that town."

—*Matthew 10:14–15* (NIV)

"Do not give dogs what is sacred; do not throw your pearls to pigs. If you do, they may trample them under their feet, and then turn and tear you to pieces."

—*Matthew 7:6* (NIV)

Before Anne Hutchinson was born, her father Francis Marbury had been thrown into English prisons three times for his Puritan views. Anne, Quaker "heretic", came by her spit honestly.

In 1630 the archbishop of Canterbury cracked down on the growing numbers of Puritans, and Anne, her husband William, and their several children were among the first to flee to the New World. To help pass the time aboard ship Anne took to holding Bible studies for the women, her leadership inadvertently upsetting some of the men. Upon investigation, the men were further upset to find Anne claiming direct communication from God through his Holy Book. Nevertheless, Anne stuck by her guns.

Once in Boston Anne and her husband quickly made a name for themselves. Within months William was a wealthy merchant, while Anne became well known for her Bible studies, which met weekly in their large home across the street from Governor John Winthrop.

Anne developed a loyal following. Not only was she adept at midwifery, nursing, and friendship, she opened new doors of intellectual thought. Husbands even began attending her Bible studies and before long eighty men and women crowded into her home, leaving many more to stand about outside—much to John Winthrop's growing dismay.

Bedrock to Puritan government was the notion of order. Anne's Bible studies were undermining that notion. Who was she, a mere woman, to interpret what only men, ministers, could understand? Winthrop sent John Wilson, the senior minister, and John Cotton, his assistant, to question Anne about her theology.

On the basis of that investigation, she was brought to trial in November 1637. When she again declared that God communicated to her directly through the Scriptures, Winthrop pronounced, "Mistress Hutchinson, the sentence of the court you hear is that you are banished from out of our jurisdiction as being a woman not fit for our society . . . "[15]

"Why, what is the charge?" she asked.

"Say no more. The court knows and is satisfied."[16]

Banishment was set for spring and William set off at once to Rhode Island in search of new land to emigrate to. Taking advantage of his absence, the church now brought her to trial. Forty-six years old, pregnant with her thirteenth child and in poor health, she was questioned *without break* for ten hours. At last John Wilson announced, "I command you in the name of Christ Jesus and of this church as a leper to withdraw your selfe out of the Congregation."[17]

Anne rose and walked stiffly to the Meeting House door. I can see her holding the small of her back, aching and sore from the pressure of her pregnancy. But I can hear the ring of conviction in her voice. "The Lord judgeth not as man judgeth," she said. "Better to be cast out of the Church than to deny Christ."[18]

Anne, nine of her children, and a few loyal followers set out on foot for Rhode Island, covering sixty miles in six days. It proved too exhausting and Anne's baby was stillborn. John Cotton smugly responded that God's punishment was justly due.

But Anne was not to be stopped. She was fighting for the right of women to read for themselves, to think and come to their own understanding of God. And women lived in Portsmouth, Rhode Island, as well as Boston, Massachusetts.

Boston was not happy. They sent a letter to William promising to forgive him if he would but denounce his wife's teachings. "I am more nearly tied to my wife than to the church," he wrote back, declining. "And I look upon her as a dear saint and servant of God."[19]

In 1642 William died, leaving Anne without support in a time when Boston was simultaneously moving to gain jurisdiction over Portsmouth *and* accusing her of witchcraft. Having no other recourse she moved into a Dutch territory on Long Island, only to find the Dutch and Indians at war. A year after William died she was killed, along with five of her six children still living at home. The Bostonian clergy and government rejoiced. "God's hand is apparently seen herein," said John Winthrop. "Proud Jezebel has at last been cast down."[20]

Anne Hutchinson fought gallantly for the right of women to seek their own personal experience with God, and for that fight she died. It appears the dragon won.

Or did it?

Last summer I visited Boston, a city rich with a history of bloodshed and contradiction. A larger-than-life statue of Anne sits on the front lawn of the government buildings. I had not expected to find her there. Had she died in vain? I wondered. Had the dragon really won?

No. As a little girl I grew up seeing in the pages of Scripture different ideas than my father did. Now a woman and I still see in the pages of Scripture different ideas than the preachers do. But no one banishes me.

I sat a long time amidst the roses planted nearby, watching the
sun glance off the proud and noble bronze jaw, and it was a comfort to me, a woman three hundred and forty-six years later, to
know that while some dragons rage, some are eventually slain.

NOT ALL DRAGONS CAN BE SLAIN, AND HEREIN LIES A DANGER
We Can Become Like Our Enemies

Do not repay anyone evil for evil. Be careful to do what is right in the eyes of everybody.

—*Romans 12:17 (NIV)*

Not all dragons can be slain. In fact, most cannot: the witches and dragons facing women today are too powerful.

"What are you going to do with my dog?" Dorothy cries when the wicked witch stuffs poor Toto into a basket. "Give him back to me!"

"Certainly. When you give me those slippers."

"But the good Witch of the North told me not to!"

"Very well. Throw that basket in the river and drown him!"

Recently I participated in a task force that was investigating gender bias in the Washington state court system. If you're a woman, says the thirteen-member panel of legislators and attorneys, and seeking justice in a court of law, you're just not going to find it.[21] Within the family women lose as well. One out of every two wives are physically assaulted by their husbands, and if you're a woman and going to be murdered, chances are you'll be killed by someone who claims to love you rather than by a stranger on the streets.[22] Historically women have lost. "Remember the women," Abigail Adams admonished when John went off to help draft the Constitution.[23] No one did. Economically women lose. The average woman college graduate earns the same as the average male high-school graduate, and women *still* only earn sixty cents for every dollar men earn.[24] When country music twangs over the radio, "Cowboys don't cry, heroes don't die," we know better. We do cry. We do die.

"You see that?" the wicked witch hisses, turning over the hour glass. "That is how long you've got to be alive! I can't wait forever to get those shoes!"

Our first temptation is to give in, to give the dragons what they want. "You can have your old slippers," we cry along with Dorothy. "But give me back Toto!"

But wait— The ruby slippers don't come off! We can't avoid the battle! We can apologize, we can beg, we can promise. We can do everything Dorothy did to convince the Witch we are throwing in the towel, but it won't work. The slippers won't come off until we're dead; and horrified, we watch as the sands of time run out.

"I'm frightened!" cries Dorothy. We are too. We can hardly think straight we're so afraid, and in our panic it's too easy to become evil ourselves.

"In the heat of the fray," Scott Peck explains, "it is tempting to take hold of some seemingly simple solution—such as 'what we ought to do is just bomb the hell out of those people.' "[25] And why not? Gretel popped the wicked old witch into the oven and Brer Rabbit smacked the tar baby for "being rude."

"If you don't say *howdy*," he'd warned, "by de time I count three, I'm goin' ter *blip* you in de nose."

Do you remember the story? The tar baby of course didn't answer and old Brer Rabbit drew back his fist and *blip!* But his fist stuck; it was tar he'd struck.

"Let go my fist!" he hollered and drew back his other fist. Stuck. It made him even madder and on and on he went, hitting and punching and finally butting his head, getting more and more tangled and looking more and more like his "enemy." "De more he try ter get unstuck-up," narrates Uncle Remus, "de stucker-up he got" until soon good old Brer Rabbit was so stuck, he "can't skacely move his eyeballs."[26]

We might excuse Gretel's desperate measure and even laugh at old Brer Rabbit, but Euripides' *Medea*, however, warns of evil more personal.

Medea had once upon a time saved Jason and proven herself a valiant Warrior. But what happened when Jason, years later, threw her over for the king's daughter? As casually as one might toss aside a soiled napkin, Jason tossed away his family, banishing

Medea along with their two little boys. Who among us can blame Medea for her rage?

We can and do, however, question Medea for what she did. John Dewey, an education philosopher, said that when we fight back "we become like those whom we oppose,"[27] and this is exactly what happened to Medea. Even though the Chorus urged her "to uphold the laws of human life—'I tell you, you must not do this!' "[28] Medea would not be stopped. Enraged with a patriarchy that supported and even applauded the disregard of wife and children, she did not care whom she brought down in her effort to punish Jason and see that justice be done. She used her sons to kill the bride and king, and then with her own hands, rather than see them die in exile, she killed her boys. Fighting for justice, she'd become as her enemy and become evil herself.

Medea is not alone. We, too, become as our enemy. The American Civil Liberties Union (ACLU), avowed Warriors for civil liberty, fights to ban certain books from state libraries, because they don't believe in religious expression. Right-wing religious groups, claiming to support the values of love and life, bomb abortion clinics. Our American democracy, founded on a belief in self-determination, fights the militance of third-world countries with a foreign policy committed to militant force. We *do* become as our enemy. How, then, do we avoid it?

By remembering *why* we as Warriors are fighting. Are we fighting to destroy or to protect? Are we, we have to ask ourselves, being shaped by our principles or are we being reshaped by our enemy?

Harriet Tubman was probably being shaped by her principles when she held her gun to the temple of any slave who wanted to turn around and go back to the South. "You go North or die," she'd say. One cashed-in ticket on the Underground Railroad would seal the doom of hundreds.[29]

I suspect Hannah Dustin, however, was being reshaped by her enemy. In 1657, after the Indians had kidnapped her and dashed her newborn infant's brains against a tree, she killed two braves, then bludgeoned to death two squaws and four children before making her escape with ten scalps tied to her waist for bounty money.[30]

When we fight back, we must ask over and over, are we being shaped by our principles? Or are we being reshaped by our enemy? We have to ask, and ask again, and then yet again. *Are we being shaped by our principles, or are we being reshaped by our enemy?* It's so easy to get disoriented and forget why we're fighting in the first place.

In the story of Deborah fighting the Canaanites, Deborah never forgot why she fought. "Village life in Israel ceased," she sang triumphantly, battle over, "until I, Deborah, arose, arose a mother to Israel." Nor did she become like her enemy, Sisera of Canaan. She simply moved in, defeated him swiftly, and pulled out. "So may your enemies perish, O Lord! But may they who love you be like the sun when it rises in its strength!"[31]

Dorothy in Oz does not forget the why of her battle either. "Run, Toto, run!" she screams, remembering even in her fright why she is fighting: to protect and defend Toto. "Run!" Out the door, down the stairs, past the guards, and off the drawbridge. "He got away!" she cries. Her voice catches. "He got away . . . "

Toto loves Dorothy too. And so do the Tinman, Scarecrow, and Lion.

"Dorothy? Are you in there? It's us!" they all ask outside the tower room where she is locked up and waiting to die.

"Yes, it's me!"

Just in time the Tinman axes the door to shreds. Dorothy throws herself into the Lion's welcoming arms.

"Hurry!" the Scarecrow urges, keeping his head about him. "It's not over yet. We've got no time to lose!" Off they go, fleeing, running, tearing down the stairs and out the—

"Going somewhere?" the Witch wants to know.

Cornered. Cut off at the pass. No hope for rescue now. No place to flee. Everyone is going to die.

"How about a little fire, Scarecrow?"

"No, no! Help! I'm burning! I'm burning! I'm burning!"

But wait— Dorothy is still a Warrior, no matter how tough the odds. Not the kind who has become like her enemy, fighting fire with fire and being shaped by the evil she hopes to combat, but a Warrior shaped by her own principles of love and protection. She fights fire with water and flings a bucket of water over the Scarecrow.

Surprising things can happen when we fight back in love.

Whenever we talk about evil, dragons, and conflict, we ultimately have to talk about love. The cruelest of dragons can only be stopped by brute force, but they can never be destroyed. This the Warrior discovers when the dragons prove too powerful. But we are not without hope, for when we start loving those around us and making choices to fight on their behalf, we find that good, through no direct action on our part, does eventually conquer evil.

"I'm melting!" screams the Witch when the water accidentally splashes onto her. "Melting . . . oh . . . " We look on aghast, stunned and unbelieving. "Who would have thought," the Witch moans, caving in on herself, evil consumed by evil, "a good little girl like you could destroy my beautiful wickedness!" Only the hat remains, and the broom.

"We realize what we dimly have always known," says Scott Peck. "Evil can be conquered only by love."[32] But not necessarily the way we've been taught.

In Madeleine L'Engle's *A Wrinkle in Time,* Meg went back to Camazotz to get her little brother, Charles Wallace, held captive and consumed by IT. Her only weapon to fight the sinister force of evil was a clue Mrs. Which had given her just before she left. *"Yyou hhave ssomethinngg ITT hhass nnott,"* the old woman had said. But Meg had to figure out what that was for herself.[33]

In direct confrontation with IT, Meg found IT couldn't get her if she fought back in anger. But wait, this was not anger anymore. This was hatred she felt—sheer unadulterated hatred. Suddenly she was lost in the breadth and scope of her hatred, and her stomach began churning in rhythm to IT. With every vestige of consciousness she jerked herself free. Hate wasn't what she had that IT didn't have! IT knew *everything* about hate!

Her little brother, twisted and consumed by IT, screamed at her, "Mrs. Whatsit hates you!" But that wasn't true. Mrs. Whatsit loved her. And suddenly she knew. Love! IT did not have love! That was her weapon!

But could she love IT? Could she love IT enough to see such evil shrivel up and die? IT surely would not be able to withstand love. Madeleine L'Engle drives home an important point about fighting evil when she writes of Meg: "But she, in all her weakness and foolishness and baseness and nothingness was incapable of loving IT. . . . But," L'Engle writes, "she could love Charles Wallace."[34]

I love you, I love you, I love you. Meg cried it out loud.

Charles Wallace's eyes stopped twirling, his forehead stopped twitching. He stepped toward her, and then suddenly he was running and shrieking, "Meg! Meg! Meg!"

"I love you, Charles! I love you!"[35]

There was a whirl of darkness and then she and Charles were home again, rolling on sweet earth. Meg, through love for her brother, had saved him.

And is this not what happened in *The Wizard of Oz?*

Dorothy was incapable of loving the witch, the evil enemy, *but she was capable of loving the Scarecrow.* And it was by loving the Scarecrow, dashing his flames, that the witch, *indirectly,* was destroyed. "She's dead," says a guard after looking at the wicked Witch of the West. "You killed her."

"I didn't mean to kill her. It's just that he was on fire . . . " It's just that Dorothy loved the Scarecrow, and evil is conquered by love.

We can't love evil, and we make a mistake if we think we can. For like Meg and Dorothy we're too weak and foolish and base and nothing; we are incapable of such love. But we can love the victims of evil. We can love Charles Wallace and the Scarecrow—and all those held in evil's power.

And when we do, the dragons are slain. In Israel, the last verse in the story of Deborah is simply, "Then the land had peace forty years." And in Oz, there is the puddle of water—and the broomstick.

"Hail, Dorothy!" A cheer goes up. Ding, dong, the wicked witch is dead!

"The broom," says Dorothy in a sudden smile to all those she's set free. "May we have it?"

And so with our broomstick in hand, proof that we've come to understand *how* love conquers evil (and cautioned not to become like our enemy), we are ready for the next step of our inner journey—the hardest task of all: transforming evil through the healing, magical role of the Wizard.

NOTES

1. M. Scott Peck, *The People of the Lie* (New York: Simon & Schuster, 1983), 68.

2. Flavius Josephus, *Life and Works.*

3. Lyle Koehler, "The Case of the American Jezebels," Linda K. Kerber and Jane DeHart-Matthews, eds., *Women's America* (New York: Oxford University Press, 1987), 52, 53.

4. Dialogue taken from Walt Disney video *Dumbo.*

5. Carol Pearson, *The Hero Within* (San Francisco: Harper & Row, 1986), 86.

6. Interview, November 1990.

7. Terry Link, "Original Red Riding Hood not a wimp, scholar reports," *The Tribune,* 8 September 19   .

8. Elizabeth Deen, *All The Women of the Bible* (San Francisco: Harper & Row, 1955), 63.

9. *Seattle Times,* 8 November 1988.

10. *U.S. Bureau of the Census Report,* P-60, no. 146, 1985.

11. Ruth Sidel, *Women & Children Last* (New York: Viking Penguin, 1986), 20–22.

12. Dennis O'Neil, *Secret Origins of the Super Heroes* (n.p., n.d.), 51.

13. O'Neil, *Super Heroes,* 52.

14. O'Neil, *Super Heroes,* 89.

15. Gail Reifert and Eugene M. Dermody, *Women Who Fought: An American History* (Reifert and Dermody, 1978), 8.

16. Reifert and Dermody, *Women Who Fought,* 8.

17. Lyle Koehler, "The Case of the American Jezebels: Anne Hutchinson and Female Agitation during the Years of Antinomian Turmoil, 1636–1640," in Linda K. Kerber and Jane DeHart-Mathews, eds., *Women's America* (New York: Oxford University Press, 1987), 59.

18. Koehler in Kerber and DeHart-Mathews, eds., *Women's America,* 59.

19. Reifert and Dermody, *Women Who Fought,* 9.

20. Reifert and Dermody, *Women Who Fought,* 9.

21. Judge H. Joseph Coleman, Chair, *Findings of the Washington State Task Force on Gender and Justice in the Courts* (Olympia, WA: 1989).

22. Lenore E. Walker, *The Battered Woman* (New York: Harper & Row, 1979), ix.

23. Reifert and Dermody, *Women Who Fought,* 25.

24. Deborah Belle, *Lives In Stress: Women and Depression* (New York: Viking Penguin, 1986), 4.

25. Peck, *People of the Lie,* 266.

26. Marion Palmer, *Walt Disney's Uncle Remus Stories* (New York: Golden Press, 1946), 11.

27. Information from V. Roy Wilbee, Ph.D., April 1990.

28. Euripides, *Medea,* 11. 700–812.

29. Reifert and Dermody, *Women Who Fought,* 44.

30. Reifert and Dermody, *Women Who Fought,* 20.

31. Judges 5:7 (NIV).

32. Peck, *People of the Lie,* 267.

33. Madeleine L'Engle, *A Wrinkle in Time* (New York: Farrar, Straus & Giroux, 1982), 203.

34. L'Engle, *A Wrinkle in Time,* 207.

35. L'Engle, *A Wrinkle in Time,* 208.

SEVEN *Wizard*

"I can transform this dragon!"

—*Abigail the Wizard*

TAMING BY NAMING
And Letting It Go

*A certain man in Maon, who had property there at Carmel,
was very wealthy. He had a thousand goats and three thousand
sheep, which he was shearing in Carmel. His name was Nabal
and his wife's name was Abigail. She was an intelligent and
beautiful woman, but her husband, a Calebite, was surly and
mean in his dealings. . . .*

*One of the servants told Nabal's wife Abigail: "David sent
messengers from the desert to give our master his greetings, but
he hurled insults at them. Yet these men were very good to us.
They did not mistreat us, and the whole time we were out in
the fields near them nothing was missing. Night and day they
were a wall around us all the time we were herding our sheep
near them. Now think it over and see what you can do,
because disaster is hanging over our master and his whole
household. He is such a wicked man that no one can talk to
him."*

Abigail lost no time.

—1 Samuel 25:2, 3, 14–18a (NIV)

An Orphan can't always ask for help, a Pilgrim can't always flee.
At times a Martyr's sacrifice doesn't subdue, a Warrior's sword
doesn't always slay. Sometimes the dragons are too big, too en-
trenched, too powerful. Like frightened little Pinocchio, we can't
outrun Monstro and we are swallowed whole. Like Cinderella,
clothed in rags and alone in the night, we weep without hope, "It's
just no use, no use at all."

So what do we do? Give up? Let the dragon win?

*But what about Jiminy Cricket? What about Tinkerbell? What
about the fairy godmother?* We forget there is yet another choice.

There is the choice for wizardry.

The Wizard transforms the dragon by naming conflict at its deepest level, the bottom-line truth—and then bringing into play creative alternatives.

"I hereby confer," says the Wizard in Oz, to the Scarecrow, "upon you the honorary degree of Th.D."

"Th.D.?" asks the Scarecrow.

"Doctor of . . . Thinkology."

Notice, the Wizard in Oz did not *give* the Scarecrow brains. The point of conflict was not brains. It was belief. The Scarecrow did not *believe* he had any. So the Wizard transformed the dilemma by naming the real problem and then conferring upon him something in which he *could* believe—a diploma.

"The sum of the square roots of any two sides of an isosceles triangle is equal to the square root of the remaining side!" Diploma in hand, the Scarecrow is at last confident enough to rattle off his version of Euclid. "Oh, joy! Rapture! I've got a brain!"

Such magic isn't easy. When we look at the fairy godmothers and Jiminy Crickets of our fairy tales, it's hard to relate. Rags into riches? Frogs into princes? Straw into gold? Puppets into boys? *Diplomas for brains?* In our experience, such miracles are few and far between, best left for someone more divine. We might as well try turning water into wine. Leave the Wizard role up to the fairy tales—or God, if he's of a mind. Yet God calls us to be Wizards, transforming dragons that can only be tamed through naming and creative response.

One of my favorite fairy tales is *The Paper Bag Princess* by Robert Munsch, a Canadian author. Princess Elizabeth and Prince Ronald were about to be married when a dragon came along and burned down the castle and took off with Prince Ronald. Elizabeth put on a paper bag (all that was left in the ashes) and set off to get Ronald back. In no time at all, following a trail of burned forests and horses' teeth, she came to the dragon's lair. But when she banged on the door, *bang-bang-bang,* a very weary dragon told her that, while he loved to eat princesses, he had already eaten a whole castle today. Could she come back tomorrow? SLAM!

BANG, BANG, BANG!

"Is it true," said Elizabeth the Wizard, "you are the smartest and fiercest dragon in the whole world? Is it true that you can burn up ten forests with your fiery breath?"

She *named* the very essence of the dragon: he burned things. And to prove it, the dragon burned fifty forests—wearing himself out so badly he hadn't enough breath left over to even "cook a meatball."

"Dragon!" she pushed, naming even further. "Is it true that you can fly around the world in just ten seconds?"

Around the world the dragon went. Ten seconds flat.

"Fantastic. Do it again!" She had the dragon in her power. Addicted to attention, prestige, and admiration, he was putty in her hands. She'd named him at his very deepest level. Around the world he went again. Twenty seconds this time, wearing himself out so completely he flopped right down and promptly fell fast asleep. She stepped over him, went into the lair, and rescued Ronald.[1]

Elizabeth won, not through the warfare of the Warrior or any of the other options open to her, but through the wisdom that comes from being a Wizard. She named the dragon at his deepest level and then came up with a creative solution. If a dragon likes to burn forests and fly around the world, he likes even more to be admired and respected. She appealed to that vanity and was able to play him right into her hands.

It's kind of a nifty thing to be able to do.

Most of us can't do this, though, because fundamental to the role of the Wizard is the belief that evil can at times be fought with nothing more than a statement of truth. Wizards never try to convert or slay. They simply name evil for what it is and then work their creative solutions around the givens.

For most of us, though, this is tantamount to condoning all that is wrong in the world. It's to allow "evil" to remain unchallenged, and we choke.

My first experience with a Wizard was when I was six years old. I was in the swamp with the ducks when a red-headed, freckle-faced kid with big ears poked a nose over the ridge and said, "Hey! We were here first."

"Pardon?"

"My pop said we were the first ones to move in around here."

"You may have been the first ones to move into the subdivision," I told him, my dander getting up, for I took great pride in being the first on Coast Meridian Road, "but when we moved here it was all woods. Where your house is," I said, climbing the ridge to point it out, "is where the bear used to live."

He wouldn't believe me, and I, incensed, went to get the authority: my father. To my surprise, my father—the authority—wasn't interested in defending the truth. "But, Daddy!" I wailed. "He says he was the first to move in and *that's not true!*"

"But you know what's true, don't you?"

"Yes."

"Isn't that enough?"

My father was the most foolish man I could ever imagine, which is exactly the way the rest of the world views Wizards. Enough? Since when is letting someone get away with being wrong, enough? That's just *letting* evil prevail!

What we don't understand is that it requires a great deal of faith to be a Wizard, faith in self—and in God. Faith to let go and trust that truth, even the truth of evil, when stated and named, can win.

"You are a lousy mother," said Fay's[2] ex-husband one day in the driveway so all the neighbors could hear. "You never take the girls to the park. You never read them bedtime stories. You never run them down to the library—"

"You're right," Fay interrupted, "I am a lousy mother."

The ex, a big, strapping kind of a guy, pushed his mouth shut, popped into his 1989 Corvette, black on black, and roared away. What else was there to do or say? Fay the Wizard had cut him off at the pass—by agreeing with his truth.

"But," a friend of mine objected when I told her the story, "she had to admit she was a lousy mother *and that's not true!*"

But wait. Fay did not admit she was a lousy mother. She simply admitted that her ex-husband *thought* she was, which was true. He did. And magically, by naming *that* truth, Fay won. Why else did the guy hot-rod away?

Wizards waste no time in childish banter. They peel back the layers of truth like peeling back the layers of an onion, smelly though it may be. They accept truth for what it is, even the truth of evil. And then trusting Christ when he says, "You shall know the truth, and the truth shall set you free,"[3] they then move quickly toward creative resolution.

This is not always so easy, for if we have a problem with letting evil go unchallenged, we *really* have a problem with creative alternatives. Which is the real reason, I think, why so few of us pursue the role of Wizard. It feels sneaky.

Jesus said, "I am sending you out like sheep among wolves. Therefore be as shrewd as snakes and as innocent as doves."[4] Nonetheless, we get nervous. Shrewd as snakes? To hold back the trump? We feel guilty when "shrewd." To be a Wizard, for a woman, is to feel profoundly guilty. Fortunately we have Abigail, a Wizard from the Old Testament, to ease our minds.

Abigail's husband, Nabal, was a rich man, but he was also a fool. Abigail had to be shrewd. After shearing season one year wicked old Nabal held a party and invited several guests. David and six hundred of his men, on the run from King Saul and camping out in nearby Maon, had helped Nabal's shepherds protect the huge flock of three thousand sheep and one thousand goats, spread for miles over the open desert. When the feasting began David sent ten of his men to ask for some provisions. It seemed an appropriate thing to do.

Nabal, however, sneered contemptuously, "Who is David? And who is the son of Jesse? Why should I take my bread and water, and the meat I have slaughtered for my shearers, and give it to men coming from who knows where?"

A servant overheard the conversation and hurried to Abigail, a woman in whom he apparently had a great deal of confidence, which would suggest that Abigail was used to cleaning up after her husband's blunders. At any rate, the servant advised her of David's request and her husband's insults. "Yet these men were good to us!" he said, breathless with fear. "Night and day they were a wall around us while we sheared the sheep. Nothing was missing when they were with us. Yet Nabal is such a wicked man no one can talk to him, and disaster hangs over us all! Please, see what you can do."

See what you can do? What *can* a woman do?

Obviously Abigail couldn't talk to her husband. The messenger had said it himself. Nabal was such a wicked man *no one* could talk to him. Could she be an Orphan? Pilgrim? Martyr? Warrior? But none of these choices offered the immediate resolution she needed. What about Wizard?

The Bible tells us Abigail lost no time. She took two hundred loaves of bread, two skins of wine, five dressed sheep, a bushel of roasted grain, a hundred cakes of raisins, and two hundred cakes of pressed figs, loaded everything onto donkeys, and took off—without so much as a boo to her drunken idiot of a husband.

When she rounded a mountainous ravine on her donkey, she came upon David and four hundred of his six hundred men, their angry voices carrying on the hot, dusty evening breeze. "It's been useless," David was saying, "all my watching over this fellow's property in the desert so that nothing of his was missing. The man's paid me back evil for good, that's what he's done, and may God deal with me, be it ever so severely, if by morning I leave alive any male of all who belong to him!"

Abigail hastened to close the gap, clippity-clop. "Whoa . . ." She quickly dismounted, then bowed before the shepherd who'd fled the wrath of King Saul. "My Lord, pay no attention to that wicked man Nabal," she said, cutting to the quick of the conflict by naming the truth. "He is just like his name—his name is Fool, and folly goes with him."

What? Call your husband a fool? This *is* going too far. There are rules against this sort of behavior. We pull out the rule book to check. Wasn't it enough she'd gone behind the man's back? And disobeyed his orders? What wife has the right to malign her husband, for whatever reason?

But Abigail was not maligning anyone. "Please," she said to David, still bowed before him. "Forgive Nabal's offense." A Wizard, she was not out to *create* trouble, but to *resolve* it. And while she did not hesitate to name the truth, neither did she condemn. She was as Christ commands us all to be, shrewd—yet innocent.

"And take this gift," she said of the food, putting the icing on the cake of her creative solution, "which I've brought, as servant to her master. Give it to the men who follow you, for the Lord will certainly make of you a lasting dynasty because you fight the Lord's battles."

A Wizard, shrewd yet innocent, Abigail saw and named the deepest level of the dilemma, her husband's folly—and then went on to seek creative alternatives, and the dragon was transformed. "Go home in peace," said David, accepting from her hand all that she brought. "I have heard your words and granted your request."

Taming by naming and letting it go is what a Wizard does. With the magic wand of truth we *can* change rags into riches, and frogs into princes, straw into gold, puppets into boys, and—

"The sum of the square roots of any two sides of an isosceles triangle is equal to the square root of the remaining side! Oh, joy! Rapture!"

—diplomas into brains.

It's not that hard to do, it just takes a little practice.

SANDI

A gentle answer turns away wrath
but a harsh word stirs up anger.

—Proverbs 15:1 (NIV)

A few summers ago a girlfriend and I went to Montreal for our summer holiday. She'd grown up in the city. I'd lived seventy miles north, up in the Laurentian Mountains, the year I was ten. For a week we prowled old Montreal, jogged Mt. Royal, shopped for bargains along Rue de St. Laurent, and drank iced tea in the outdoor Sir Winston Churchill pub. At the end of the week I called for a car rental and the two of us headed downtown to pick it up.

"Oh," the woman at the desk told me, "we don't have that model anymore. But we do have the four-door Grand Prix . . ." You guessed it. They'd pulled a fast one and I had to either fork over twice the money I'd been quoted or forget my trip to the Laurentians. I hit the ceiling. The woman at the desk and I locked into verbal combat, and I lost. Sandi and I were not going to the Laurentians after all and I was livid.

Sandi, though, popped into high gear, pulling out of her hat all the old Wizard tricks. *"Excusez mon amie, si'l vous plaît, mais . . ."* I stood stunned, watching her in action. She went straight to the heart of the matter, naming it for what it was in a soft and gentle voice. I had called. A reservation for a two-door Mazda had been placed. The price had been confirmed. So far so good. But then Sandi switched gears. *"Peut-être mon amie ne comprende pas,"* she said. Wait a minute, *I didn't understand?* She was exonerating the rental agency that had tried to rip me off. Her soft and gentle voice melted their wrath quickly, although it left me feeling a bit blistered. But I came out of my slow boil when Sandi instructed me in English to thank them nicely for the four-door Grand Prix they were willing to give me for the same price as the compact Mazda. *How had she done it?*

I quickly apologized. *"Merci beaucoup, très bien!"* I said. I grabbed the keys and Sandi and I took off for the Laurentians before the agency could figure out what I'd been hollering about in the first place. "What happened?" I asked, dodging Montreal drivers and wondering if I'd paid for any insurance on this Grand Prix.

"I let them save face by pointing the finger at you," said Sandi the Wizard, kind enough, though, not to point out I heartily deserved it. "They were so mad at you," she went on, "Oops! WATCH OUT FOR THAT GREEN CAR! I knew they'd rather see you set back a peg or two than lose your $24.95 by showing you the door." She jabbed a finger out the front window, signaling the exit sign I'd been looking for. *The Laurentians.* "I just gave them what they wanted—you in a skillet!"

Sandi named the truth (my reservations and behavior), found a creative response (serving me up in a frying pan!), and *voilà!* One dragon down and one feeling a little sheepish, for Sandi was a Wizard who could transform two dragons at a time.

JOCHEBED

> *Then Pharaoh gave this order to all his people: "Every boy that is born you must throw into the Nile, but let every girl live."*
> —*Exodus 1:22 (NIV)*

Jochebed was born with her wits about her. She was the mother of Aaron, first of the Hebrew priesthood, Miriam, first of Hebrew prophets, and Moses, first of Hebrew military leaders. These three children of hers were the founders of the Hebrew nation, uniting the remnant of Abraham, Isaac, and Jacob with a code of laws, religious structure, and a national identity. And while not much is known about Jochebed, we know of her children, and we know of her incredulous act of wizardry on a day when the dragon roared.

The Hebrews were growing strong in Egypt, and so the Pharaoh, threatened by their sheer numbers, ordered all baby boys born to Hebrew women be thrown into the river. We only have to think of *Crocodile Dundee* to know the fate of these tiny babies still wrinkled and pink from birth, and as Zora Hurston Neale,

Afro-American folklorist, says in her novel, *MOSES Man Of The Mountain,* "A great force of suffering accumulated between the basement of heaven and the roof of hell."[5]

The suffering snared the heart of Jochebed when she looked into the wee face of her third child, for she could not bear to see him tossed to crocodiles. But how could she save him? How?

For three months she kept him hidden, perhaps in a barn where his cries might mingle with the squawk of chickens and the braying of a donkey. Perhaps she kept him in a root cellar, in a cradle wedged between clay jars filled with grain, peppercorns, onions, bread, and dates, his cries muffled by the solidly packed earth above him. But she couldn't go on hiding him forever, and night and day she prayed. "Oh, God of Abraham, Isaac, and Jacob, look upon your servant with compassion."

I think she must have been asleep when the answer finally came, for the answer is not one the conscious mind ferrets out. The river! If the dragon was throwing babies to the Nile, what safer place could there be? If that's what the dragon wanted, so be it. If God was of a mind, Jochebed thought, the basket she would make might float to kinder people who would hear her baby's feeble cries and take him in.

The next morning, hope surging for the first time in her breast, Jochebed instructed Miriam and Aaron to quickly fetch her some reeds from the riverbank to weave a basket boat. "I want only the papyrus! Nothing else will do, for papyrus keeps off them crocodiles!" And off scampered Aaron and Miriam.

She wove the basket tight, lined it with pitch and tar, and then with a prayer to a God who had not spoken in four hundred years she put in goose feathers and a sheeting made from the skirt of one of her own dresses. She nursed her son for the last time and, when he was asleep, laid him inside. Did she hesitate to close the lid? Did she falter when she set the basket into the river? Did she set her face and seal her heart when she had to give a wee push, to let the current take him from her? According to Zora Neale Hurston, she said, "Youse such a great big river and he is such a little bitty thing. Show him some mercy, please."[6]

We all know the story of mercy: how Pharoah's own daughter came out to bathe and heard his cries, how she ordered the basket be fetched, and how she took one look at him and with compassion said, "This is one of the Hebrew babies." We all know how

Miriam, hiding among the bullrushes, was quick witted enough to dash out and say, "Shall I go and get one of the Hebrew women to nurse the baby for you?" And we all know how Moses was nursed by his own mother, raised in Pharaoh's court, and how years later it was he who led his people out from Pharaoh's land.

But we forget Jochebed, mother of Aaron, Miriam, and Moses—and a Wizard who transformed a dragon.

TAMAR

If brothers are living together and one of them dies without a son, his widow must not marry outside the family. Her husband's brother shall take her and marry her and fulfill the duty of a brother-in-law to her. The first son she bears shall carry on the name of the dead brother so that his name will not be blotted out from Israel.

—Deuteronomy 25:5 (NIV)

Married to one of Judah's evil sons slain by the Lord for his wickedness, Tamar was quickly married off according to leviratic law to his brother. But he too was evil and was slain by God. Judah promised Tamar his third son, as soon as Shelah was of age, so that she might have a son.

Judah, however, delayed the ceremony with one excuse after another, fearful that Shelah too might die. He harbored the notion that there was something sinister about Tamar. It was *her* fault, he decided, that his other two sons were dead. This left Tamar in a real bind, for leviratic law forbade her marriage outside the family, and yet by the same law she was guaranteed a son. And she needed a son. A son was equivalent to a retirement fund. So what was she to do? It seems like an odd law to us and hardly fair, but nonetheless Tamar, an apparently devout woman, abided by it. She remained unmarried and waited patiently for Judah to make good, although it was evident he never intended to.

Tamar was not one to sit idle, however, twiddling her thumbs forever while waiting around for dragons to see reason. When

Judah's wife died she devised a plan that would force old Judah to accept his responsibility. It was sheep shearing season, and guests and Judah were out and about, passing back and forth on the roads of Timnath. Wrapping herself in a colorful and becoming robe and drawing a veil over her face to completely disguise herself, she went out to the road and waited.

Judah thought she was a prostitute and propositioned her.

For a fee, she said.

What fee? He offered a kid goat.

Give me a pledge until it is sent, she told him.

What kind of pledge?

Oh, your signet, your bracelets, and your staff will do.[7]

He must have been really taken with her to agree. They went into a tent and she conceived. She went home, took off her apparel, and resumed the dress of widowhood. Judah, in the meantime, sent his servant with the kid into the town where she lived with orders to bring back his more personal belongings.

"Where is the harlot?" the servant asked at the village outskirts and the townsmen exclaimed, "Harlot? Why, there is no harlot here!"

Three months later Judah heard that Tamar was "with child by whoredom." Typical of those who break the law when it doesn't suit them, he was quick to enforce the law when it did. "Bring her here," he said, "so that she might be burned!" I can't help but wonder if this isn't what he'd wanted to do all along, convinced as he was that it was Tamar's evil that had destroyed his wicked sons. At any rate, Tamar appeared before him and knocked his socks off.

"Discern, I pray thee," she said, holding out his signet, bracelets, and staff, "whose are these?"

He could not deny the truth, for it was as plain as the nose on his face. "She's been more righteous than I," he said, "because I wouldn't give her Shelah my son."

In due time Tamar bore Judah twin sons, one of them Pharez, ancestor of King David. It would not have happened, though, had she not chosen the role of Wizard. She named the dragon for who he was, an unfair and callous old man, and devised a creative alternative by making im acknowledge *his* sin, thereby transforming the dragon who thought he had won.

SCHOOL PRINCIPAL

The purposes of a man's heart are deep waters,
but a man of understanding draws them out.

—*Proverbs 20:5* (NIV)

A professor used to tell this story to his Ph.D. candidates at some point in their graduate work in education at the University of Michigan, and it illustrates perfectly what a Wizard is.

An elementary student, so the story goes and who shall remain nameless (but who probably holds many names), was once a straight-A whiz. But suddenly, almost overnight, he started getting only Cs. The teacher tried everything she knew, but to no avail. The puzzled and exasperated teacher sent the student down to the principal's office. As it turned out, the student confessed that kids made fun of her for her exemplary marks.

This story reminds me of my son coming home on the last day of third grade, report card under arm. Some bully on the playground had shrieked, "There goes Blake! He's so dumb! He didn't get any pluses!" Blake, cut to the very quick, for he's a very bright boy, climbed up on the corner desk in my office and was crying out all his troubles to his big brother, Phillip.

"And they all started to laugh!" Blake blubbered, truly bruised by the misnaming. "And I tried to tell them I got *all* pluses except two, and they were check pluses, and—"

Just then Heather, who had graduated from middle school and would begin high school in the fall, passed by. "That's okay, Blake," she said, giving him a tender pat on the back. "This year they'll tease you for low grades. In a few years they'll be teasing you for high ones."

I'm not sure why the puzzled teacher in the story hadn't figured it out, if a graduating eighth grader understands the great dragon of "higher education." The smarter you are, the more of an oddball you are, and in this particular story, fortunately, the principal understood. She also understood, as does every Wizard, that there's not much point in trying to argue about it.

So rather than argue, rather than try to convert the dragon or subdue it or slay it, or force any kind of issue with it, the principal simply pulled out a blank report card. She signed it and handed it over to the student.

"Here," she said. "Fill this out with any grades you want and show it to your friends. But straighten up and we'll keep the real report card in my office. A deal?"

The principal recognized the truth and responded with a creative alternative, and the dragon was transformed.

NARRATOR OF CRANFORD

Do not say, "I'll pay you back for this wrong!"
Wait for the Lord, and he will deliver you.

—Proverbs 20:22 (NIV)

When Miss Matty in *Cranford* was shopping for a new gown, she overheard a farmer's disbelief that his bank note was being turned down. The Town and County Bank, he was being told, was about to fail and no store was accepting funds from that source. But the farmer had spent some time trying to decide on just the right shawl for his lady and was thunderstruck to be told he had to put it back.

Miss Matty hurried over, questioning the whole transaction. What was wrong with a note from the Town and County Bank? she wanted to know. Why, she was a shareholder at the bank and she would have, she was sure, heard if there had been any trouble.

Very well, if you insist, she said, digging into her purse. She would give the farmer five sovereigns to cover his note and get his scarf. She would look into the matter.

But the owner of the store warned her not to. You, Miss Matty, Mr. Johnson confided, are without funds as well if you hold shares in the Town and County.

"Perhaps so," she told him. "But I don't pretend to understand business; I only know that if it is going to fail, and if honest people are to lose their money because they have taken our notes—I can't explain myself. . . . Only I would rather exchange my gold for the note, if you please." Here she turned to the farmer. "And then you can take your wife the shawl. It is only going without my gown a few days longer. Then, I have no doubt, everything will be cleared up."[8]

"But if it is cleared up the wrong way?" asked the narrator, a young woman two generations younger than the elderly spinster, and through whose eyes the story is told.

It *was* cleared up the wrong way. Miss Matty's bank was broke. Miss Matty was ruined.

In this delightful novel of the mid-nineteenth century, Elizabeth Gaskell, a minister's wife, weaves a complex tapestry of wizardry at its best—so that we can see just how the repayment of good, rather than evil, can bring about a solution to an impossible problem: what *can* Miss Matty do to support herself?

The narrator says: "I thought of all the things by which a woman, past middle age, and with the education common to ladies fifty years ago, could earn or add to a living, without materially losing caste . . . " You see, this was the problem: how to support yourself without losing caste in English society.

Teaching, of course, was the first thing to present itself to the narrator. Piano, perhaps, to children. But no, "that faint shadow of musical acquirement had died out years before." Needlework? No, "Miss Matty's eyes were failing her." Geography? Horrors! Equators and tropics and mysterious circles were imaginary lines to Miss Matty who "looked upon the signs of the Zodiac as so many remnants of the Black Art." Ah! Candle lighters or "spills," as Miss Matty preferred to call the knit garters. But alas, teaching such a skill could do nothing but "distress her sense of propriety."

There was nothing, thought the narrator, "she could teach to the rising generation of Cranford." But then the tea-urn was brought in for afternoon tea and a new thought entered the narrator's head. Why should Miss Matty not be an agent for the East India Tea Company? There could be no objections to the plan, for tea was neither greasy nor sticky, two qualities Miss Matty could not abide. Nor was tea too heavy, taxing Miss Matty's fragile strength. The only problem was the license. To trade, to buy and sell, was a degradation, and the required license was a serious flaw in the plan.

But! thought the narrator, the license could be put in a spot where no one could see it!

And so it was. Miss Matty's parlor was turned into a tea house, without the degrading characteristics of trade: instead of a counter there was a table; there were comfits and lozenges to tempt the children in; and there were bright canisters for the tea itself. The floorboards were scrubbed to a white cleanness and adorned with a brilliant piece of oilcloth for the customers to stand upon while waiting at the table-counter. And the license? "A very small 'Matilda Jenkyns, licensed to sell tea,' was hidden under the lintel of the new door . . . "

But wait. Miss Matty was upset. If she sold tea, she thought, it would injure Mr. Johnson's business. Down to his store she returned, to tell him of the project. But Mr. Johnson kindly put to rest all Miss Matty's concerns, any fear she might have of injuring his business. In fact, he even referred his customers to her, for his tea, he declared, was only a common tea, while Miss Matty's? Choice sorts, he assured them all.

And so Miss Matty's future was secured, her ruin behind her. Even the approval of Mrs. Jamieson, self-appointed leader of Cranford society, was gained. Miss Matty would not, she pronounced, by selling tea forfeit her right to the privileges of society in Cranford.

All's well that ends well, Elizabeth Gaskell would suggest. But, before the novel concludes, the minister's wife goes even further. Miss Matty's long lost brother, Peter, returns from India a rich man and Miss Matty lives happily ever after. The tea house is converted back into a parlor, and the ladies of Cranford continue to visit, drinking tea in the late afternoon, and protecting the structure and family life of all the town's inhabitants.

"Ever since that day," concludes Gaskell through the voice of the narrator, "there has been the old friendly sociability in Cranford society; which I am thankful for, because of my dear Miss Matty's love of peace and kindliness."

But I add, there is restoration *because the narrator made a choice for wizardry.* She, by naming the truth and seeking a creative alternative, managed to transform the mighty dragon of English sensibility.

CORRIE

*There is neither Jew nor Greek, slave nor free, male nor female,
for you are all one in Christ Jesus. If you belong to Christ, then
you are Abraham's seed, and heirs according to the promise.*
            —*Galatians 3:28–29* (NIV)

When times are hard there is never any debate: women are equal.
In colonial America when survival was dependent upon long hours
and hard work, women enjoyed a great deal of freedom and were
called deputy husbands. During the Revolutionary War they managed the farms, signed contracts, bought and sold—only to lose
their independence when the men won theirs.

In frontier America women saddled horses and rode them
astride; they owned land, chopped trees, managed businesses, and
manned the shops—only to lose their independence when civili-
zation arrived.

At the turn of the century women rode the circuit, built
churches, preached, and baptized their followers, many of them
ordained and commissioned by D. L. Moody—only to lose their
independence when the churches were established.

During World War II women went to work and earned a man's
salary while simultaneously raising families and were applauded
for their heroism—only to lose their independence and high
wages when the men came home.

There is no arguing the fact that when times are tough, when
their strength, fortitude, wisdom, talents, and insights are needed,
women are equal. But the minute things settle down? All kinds of
blocks go up to keep women down.

None of this, however, ever bothered Corrie ten Boom. It was
never even an issue with her, and when people tried to make it an
issue she simply pulled out her Wizard's wand. The story I like
best is of a run-in she once had with the Brethren Assembly: the
Brethren would not allow her to speak under the very strict scriptural interpretation that women should keep silent in the church.

This, however, did not slow Corrie down one iota. Without
bothering to argue about it, or to point out her own scriptural
support for equality, or defend what she believed God had called

her to do, she simply invited all the Sisters of the church to come hear her speak—and then invited the Brethren, saying that if they were interested in hearing what she had to say to the Sisters that week, they were more than welcome to attend. They did.

Corrie named the truth of the conflict, disagreement over scriptural interpretation, and then carried on with what God had intended her to do anyway—without ruffling any of the Brethren's feathers. And for one week at least, the dragon was transformed.

KAREN

I will lead the blind by ways they have not known,
   along unfamiliar paths I will guide them
I will turn the darkness into night before them
   and make the rough places smooth.
These are the things I will do;
   I will not forsake them.　　　　　*—Isaiah 42:16 (NIV)*

Karen Campbell knew God wanted her to marry Marc Watson, but her father didn't know that. For Karen it was a bit of a dilemma; her father wasn't a Christian, and so how was she going to resolve this one?

"How's he going to support you?" her father wanted to know. "He's a cook."

"He's got a good job," Karen pointed out. "And he's interested in getting a degree in business administration."

"He can't earn enough money in food services to raise a family," her father persisted, and she felt her dander getting up.

"*I* have a job," she told him.

"I don't like the idea of you working."

The issue, Karen realized, was not Marc. It was money. And so she thanked her father for his concern and opened her Bible to a favorite verse, Isaiah 42:16: *I will lead the blind by ways they have not known, along unfamiliar paths I will guide them; I will turn the darkness into light before them and make the rough places smooth. These are the things I will do; I will not forsake them.* Clearly this disagreement between her and her dad was something Karen was unfamiliar with, the two of them at logger-heads over something so important. They'd always been close and she had no intention of breeching the special bond they shared. But what to do? How was God to lead her through this one? But wait, she thought. I'm a banker! If it's finances he's concerned about, why not ease his mind and give him a financial statement? With her favorite Bible verse leading the way, Karen set to work, and when it was done, she handed it to her father. God, she knew, would just have to smooth out the rough places.

It wasn't the spectacular turnaround on her father's part that she'd hoped for. He was still unsure how it would all work out, but it was clear he did want the best for Karen. "The best," she insisted, "is to marry Marc."

The wedding was what was spectacular. Her father, taking her arm to begin walking her down the aisle, looked into her face and she saw that he was crying, and smiling. "Marc's a great guy," he said, "and I love you."

And so Karen was married and the conflict resolved, because she named the basic issue (money, not Marc) and had offered a creative response (a financial statement). It took a bit of time, but nonetheless the dragon was transformed.

ANNE WITH AN "E"

"Therefore, if you are offering your gift at the altar and there remember that your brother has something against you, leave your gift there in front of the altar. First go and be reconciled to your brother; then come and offer your gift."

—Matthew 5:23, 24 (NIV)

A fortnight after Anne (with an "e") arrived at Green Gables and the home of Marilla and Matthew Cuthbert, Mrs. Rachel Lynde dropped by to meet the young orphan. Anne came running in all disheveled, and Mrs. Lynde said, "Well, they didn't pick you for your looks." Skinny, homely, freckles. Hair as red as carrots.

With a bound the young orphan crossed the kitchen, her body all atremble. "I hate you!" she cried. "How dare you call me skinny and ugly! How dare . . . " On and on she stormed, stamping her foot, crying out in fury at being called redheaded and freckled. Mrs. Lynde wouldn't like if someone called her clumsy and fat and without a bit of imagination, now would she?[9]

Marilla, of course, insisted that Anne apologize. Anne, of course, would have none of it, and Marilla locked her up in her room to reconsider. Anne buckled down to a lifetime of solitary confinement. She was *not* sorry!

The next evening after the milking, though, Marilla and Anne were on their way down the lane. E. M. Montgomery tells us that one walked erect and triumphant, the other drooped and dejected, but halfway to the Lynde home suddenly Anne perked up. Marilla wanted to know what Anne was thinking. Anne was thinking, she said, of what she would say to Mrs. Lynde and Marilla began feeling like something was going just a little bit askew.

The moment they were in sight of Rachel Lynde knitting by her kitchen window Anne turned instantly penitent and mournful. She dropped to her knees, held out her hands beseechingly to the astonished woman, and cried, "I am so extremely sorry. I could never express all my sorrow, no, not if I used up a whole dictionary." And on and on she went, chastising herself and begging for forgiveness until quite suddenly the heart of Mrs. Rachel Lynde, that gossipy, cold busybody, turned quite over.

It was quite all right, she assured Anne, forgiving her instantly, admitting her own outspokenness, even adding that once she'd had a school friend whose carrot-red hair had turned a lovely auburn, and perhaps Anne's would too. Anne pulled in a long breath, rose to her feet, and said that now she had hope, that it would be so much easier to bear if her hair might someday turn a handsome auburn, and from now on she would feel as if Mrs. Lynde were her benefactor.

On the way home Anne said to Marilla, "I apologized pretty well, didn't I? I thought since I had to do it, I might as well do it thoroughly."

Marilla couldn't figure out why she felt a need to scold Anne for apologizing so well, but then that was ridiculous, wasn't it? A scolding for apologizing well? She kept back her misgivings and instead said she hoped Anne would not have to apologize for anything for a long time to come.

"Oh, Marilla," said Anne, slipping her hand into Marilla's, "I'm so happy. I could pray right now and not find it a bit difficult."[10]

Anne (with an "e") was only an Orphan, but she was also a Wizard. If the dragon wanted an apology, she figured while walking down the lane, give the dragon an apology. It'll transform the dragon every time.

M A

Give thanks in all circumstances, for this is God's will for you in Christ Jesus.

—*1 Thessalonians 5:18* (NIV)

"The blackbirds are in the corn," Laura Ingalls told Ma. "Oughtn't I tell Pa?"[11]

Ma said no, blackbirds always ate a little corn, but by noon the blackbirds were eating a *lot* of corn. Pa tried shooting them. Ma and the girls tried running up and down the rows. Pa said he'd go into town and get some more cartridges, and Ma and the girls screeched and shouted and flapped their arms until sweat ran down their backs and corn leaves cut their faces. But still the swarm of blackbirds kept eating. "It's no use, girls," said Ma.

Pa came home with the cartridges and all afternoon he shot the blackbirds. But the more he shot, the more there were. They seemed to come in from all over the Territory: common blackbirds, yellow-headed blackbirds, blackbirds with red heads and a bit of red on the wing. Hundreds of them came as if invitations had gone out, and by the next morning a dark cloud of blackbirds rested over the cornfield. The crop's gone, said Pa. We might as well eat what we can.

Ma sent Laura and Carrie out to pick what was left. They fought blackbirds that battered their sunbonnets, boiled what they salvaged, sliced the cobs clean, and then laid the milky kernels out on a cloth in the sun to dry, with another cloth over them to keep off the birds. Next winter they would have at least some of the corn to eat.

"Comb your hair and sit up to the table, Charles," Ma said to Pa when he came in to dinner, and she opened the oven door.

"Chicken pie?"

"Sing a song of sixpence—" Ma started to sing.

Laura and Carrie joined in, "—A pocket full of rye,"

> Four and twenty blackbirds
> Baked in a pie!
> When the pie was opened
> The birds began to sing
> Wasn't that a dainty dish
> To set before the king?

"Well, I'll be switched!" said Pa as he cut into the great big pie. They all agreed it beat chicken pie all hollow.

"It takes you to think up a chicken pie," said Pa to Ma, "a year before there's chickens to make it with."

It wasn't even Sunday and they were eating like kings. And as long as the blackbirds kept up and the garden held out, they would be eating like kings every day. "Ma is right," thought Laura, "there is always something to be thankful for."

That is, if you're a Wizard. "It's no use, girls," Ma had said when they were all sweaty and scratched from chasing off blackbirds while Pa went into town to get more cartridges. And it was. She'd named the truth but found a creative alternative. And the dragon was transformed.

NAMING OUR OWN SIN
Truth That Transforms

*"Do not judge, or you too will be judged. For in the same way
you judge others, you will be judged, and with the measure
you use, it will be measured to you.*

*"Why do you look at the speck of sawdust in your brother's
eye and pay no attention to the plank in your own eye? How
can you say to your brother, 'Let me take the speck out of your
eye,' when all the time there is a plank in your own eye? You
hypocrite, first take the plank out of your own eye, and then
you will see clearly to remove the speck from your brother's
eye."*

*"Ask and it will be given you; seek and you will find; knock
and the door will be opened to you. For everyone who asks
receives; he who seeks finds; and to him who knocks, the door
will be opened."*

—Matthew 7:1–5, 7, 8 (NIV)

The Wizard in Oz was not very nice when we first met him.
"You dare to come to me for a heart, do you?" he had mocked
the Tinman. "You clinkety, clanking, clattering collection of col-
lagenous junk!" The second time we see him, when Dorothy and
her friends returned with the wicked witch's broomstick, he is no
better. "WHY" he bellows in a perfect rage, "HAVE YOU COME
BACK?"

I'm not sure how Dorothy found her tongue. But she did. "We'd
like you to keep your promise to us," she said, "if you please, sir."

"Go away and come back tomorrow!"

"If you were really so great and powerful you'd keep your
promises!"

"DO YOU PRESUME TO CRITICIZE THE GREAT OZ?"

No, he is not a nice person, but then neither are we.

As Orphan, Pilgrim, Martyr, and Warrior, always thrown against the dragons, it's easy to begin viewing life from a "them/us" perspective. *Them* is bad, *us* is good. The Wizard, though, moves beyond this dualism to see that we are all checkered by both good and evil, them *and* us. We, too, live outside the Garden of Eden. We, too, are not without our own sin.

Abigail from the Old Testament understood this, for she prefaced her plea to David by saying, "My lord, let the blame be on me alone."[12] If there are dragons without, there are dragons within, and the Wizard is not one who allows herself to be deceived. Like Abigail, she names first her own dragon before naming—and transforming—anyone else's.

"You hypocrite!" said Jesus, affirming this truth. "First take the plank out of your own eye, and then you will see clearly to remove the speck from your brother's eye."

Easier said than done. We are skilled at self-deception. In fact, our capacity for self-deception, writes Cornelius Plantiga, Jr., "is almost fathomless."[13]

One reason for this is that both our culture and Christianity require collective conformity to defined ideals. "We are," says Carol Pearson, "supposed to 'live up' to standards of virtue, achievement, intelligence, and physical attractiveness. If we do not, then we are expected to repent, work harder, study, diet, exercise, and wear better clothes until we fit the prevailing image of the ideal person."[14] We learn early that anything or anyone less than perfect is cut from the team and so we work very, very hard to attain and maintain the prescribed ideal. Just watch everyone file out of the bank building downtown at five o'clock on a weeknight or out of church on Sunday at noon. Penguin suits, briefcase or Bible, practiced smiles. The projected image *is* what counts and so we systematically repress and pretend in order to make the team. But we're not perfect, and so we become both deceiver and deceived, our own dupes, unable anymore to see the plank in our eye.

What plank? Where? we ask. Like the Wizard in Oz, unable to admit our humanness, our good *and* bad, we retreat instead behind a curtain of self-righteousness where, when pressed, we can present a pious image created especially for public viewing. What we fail to realize is that for all the perfection we project, we, like the Wizard in Oz, are impotent, and dragons reign.

Fortunately for the Wizard, Toto is not deceived. He pulls back the self-righteous curtain and exposes the Wizard for who he is, a mere man frantically pulling levers and twisting knobs, bellowing away, "The great Oz has spoken!"

But what of us? Who pulls back our curtain? Who points out the plank we can't see so we can get on with the business of being a Wizard?

A psychological phenomenon occurs whenever we deny the truth about ourselves. Whatever we deny gets projected onto someone (or something) else. It's called "mirroring," and this is what Christ was getting at in Matthew 7. The speck reflects the plank. As Orphan, Pilgrim, Martyr, and Warrior, we see dragons as something to be conquered and tamed, but as Wizard we come to see dragons as a mirror, very often nothing more than a reflection of what is wrong in our own lives; by looking into our brother's eye, who's sin we *can* see, we are able to see reflected back at us our own sin—which we *can't* see.

It can work on a very simple level. Last week I wouldn't do something my fifteen-year-old daughter wanted done, and so she called me immature. "Immature!" I screamed. And then I let her have it, about as immaturely as anyone can.

It can work on a more complex level. My credit union filed bankruptcy, taking with it all the money I had in the world. As a single mother with three kids, fluctuating child support, and miserably high medical costs every month, I was absolutely dependent upon that money. Yet the dragon roared and I was left with nothing.

But the speck reflects the plank, and after crying in my soup for a while, I realized that the problem was not so much the end of all my money, but the absence of any trust in God to see me through.

It can also work on a very deep level, striking at the very core of who we are. One night I nearly killed my ex-husband, but the event so frightened me I denied all memory of any rage to kill. It wasn't long, though, before I'd become convinced it was *he* who wanted to kill *me*. All perspective and truth were lost because I had not yet learned we project what we deny. I didn't know it was my own evil I saw reflected in his life. I looked at him and saw only one dragon—and it wasn't me I saw.

Several years later something rekindled that rage and I was swept back to a night I'd long repressed from memory. The brutal truth hit me between the eyes. It was not he who wanted to kill me . . . but I, him. The speck reflects the plank; I'd been looking at my own dragon.

It was Pogo who said, "We have met the enemy, and the enemy is us." The enemy *is* us. We are not very nice people.

"Who *are* you?" Dorothy demands.

"I am the great and powerful Oz—" But we're not. We're not great. We're not powerful. We're just human beings, far from perfect. And we had better face the truth of it.

"You *humbug!*" the Scarecrow accuses.

"Yes, yes, it's exactly so," we finally confess. We are humbugs. We really are.

Oddly enough, this is where, in *The Wizard of Oz,* the story turns around: at the point of confession. The moment the Wizard names the plank and confesses to being a humbug, he suddenly, magically, moves out of impotent pretension into the wise and wonderful Wizard we'd set out originally to seek, able at last to name and transform conflict that before he'd been unable to even identify. Diplomas for brains, medals for courage, testimonials for hearts—even a hot-air balloon ride back to Kansas for Dorothy. There is magic, it seems, in confession.

Do you remember the story, *The Frog Prince?* The little princess lost her golden ball down the well, and an ugly old frog came along and said he'd fetch it for her—if she promised to let him eat off her golden plate and sleep on her golden pillow. "Yes, yes," she promised, but when he brought the ball she found she couldn't go through with it. He was such an *ugly* frog.

Her father told her she must. A promise was a promise. What mattered, in the king's book, was that she attain and maintain the prescribed ideal of virtue as subscribed to by our culture. It didn't matter that her own truth contradicted.

In recent versions of the story the princess complied. She kissed the frog and he turned into a handsome prince. The original version, however, is more in line with the role of Wizard. Disgusted, the little princess picked up the ugly old frog and threw him at the fire. POOF! *Then* he turned into the handsome prince!

The Bible says that if we say we have no sin, we deceive ourselves, and the truth is not in us. But! if we confess our sins, he is faithful and just to forgive us our sins, and to cleanse us from all unrighteousness.[15] Kissing the frog, denying our repulsion, doesn't work: we only deceive ourselves. But if we confess the truth, "Ugh! I *hate* ugly old frogs!" the unprecedented occurs. Frogs turn into princes, rags into riches, straw into gold. Confession leads to forgiveness, and magic and miracles are unleashed into our lives. "Old things are passed away, behold, all things are become new."[16] Forgiven, we're able, like the Wizard in Oz, to magically name and transform the evil around us—both in ourselves and others, for it's honesty, not perfection, that enables us to become the Wizards God has called us to be.

We hear all the time of drug addicts who convert to Christianity and never need another fix, of mothers who find victory in the face of a child's death, of families whose finances turn around when they begin to tithe. Testimony nights at church always abound with stories of the Wizard and great books are written every day about Wizards who transform. No one argues the truth of this; the evidence is all around. But, does it always work this way? I mean, really? Does confession and naming of truth *always* bring us everything we want and need, transforming *all* our pain into joy?

What about the chain smoker in the back pew whose fingers just itch to pick up another cigarette? The mother who can't love her teenager? Marriages that don't heal? Paralyzing grief that won't go away? What about you? Me? What about all of us who still live in the ashes of the dragon's fire?

We make a mistake when we assume *all* dragons can be transformed. They can't. And to think so is naive, perhaps even wishful thinking on our part, for how can we forget those dragons we confront as Orphan, Pilgrim, Martyr, and Warrior? Dragons that must be subdued, slain, sacrificed to, and even run from? The Wizard in us can transform a million dragons, but there's always going to be another immune to a Wizard's wand.

In *The Paper Bag Princess,* while Princess Elizabeth managed to transform the one dragon, flattering him into exhaustion, she immediately met up with another that *couldn't* be transformed: Prince Ronald himself. Prince Ronald was not impressed by Princess Elizabeth. Her hair, he said, was a mess. She was wearing a paper bag and she smelled all sooty. He told her to come back when she looked like a *real* princess. Tell me, what does a Wizard do with this?

Elizabeth told Ronald he looked like a prince, his hair all neat, his clothes all tidy, but, she said, he was a bum. They didn't get married after all. One dragon she transformed, another she abandoned—without missing a beat. And this is what a Wizard does. We roll with the punches and carry on.

Easy to say, harder to do. It's not easy to roll when we can't see the punch, and we all know what it's like when tragedy strikes. Few of us, then, are up to fairy tales and pat answers.

In *Jubilee,* Margaret Walker's historical novel about her great-grandmother, we follow Vyry through slavery, civil war, and re-construction, numbed by page after page of brutality and violence. When Vyry's own husband raises a whip against her son, she goes into a tailspin of despair. How is she to carry on?

My parents for three and a half years watched a daughter die from a congenital heart defect. Then they had to watch my fifteen-year-old brother lie paralyzed for seven weeks, neck broken from a diving accident. How were they to carry on?

Robin Bend[17] had to sit day after day in a trial against her ex-husband for raping her son, listening to the evidence and tes-timonies of doctors from the Sexual Assault Center at the Univer-sity of Washington, only to get a verdict of not guilty. Bobby was considered an unreliable witness; he was only four years old. How was she to carry on?

You, me, how do we carry on?

In *The Wizard of Oz* how is Dorothy to carry on? The Wizard is finally going to take her home, back to Kansas in his hot-air balloon! All systems are go, everyone's gathered round! At last she is off!

But, wait! Toto jumps out! She scrambles after him. "Wait for me! I'll be right back!" she calls over her shoulder.

But the balloon lifts off anyway. "Oh!" she screams. "Come back! Come back! Don't go without me! Please come back!"

"I can't come back!" the Wizard yells. "I don't know how it works!"

As Wizard we don't know everything. Let's face it, there are so many things we *don't* understand.

"Oh, no!" poor Dorothy cries, "I'll never get home!"

How do any of us carry on?

I don't know. There are no easy answers. But I think it's interesting that Jesus, right after he called us all hypocrites and told us to get the planks out of our eyes, said, "Ask and it will be given you; seek and you will find; knock and the door will be opened to you." In case we didn't get it the first time, he repeated it. "For everyone who asks receives; he who seeks finds; and to him who knocks, the door will be opened."

"What am I going to do?" asks Dorothy.

John Fischer, songwriter and musician, says, "I ask because I don't know the answer; I seek because there's more to find; I knock because this door goes somewhere."[18] And this is how we carry on. We ask. We seek. We knock. Because we do find answers, we do discover, and we do have doors opened. We do.

Do you remember Heidi? Grandmamma Sesamann had told her God always answers our prayers. But Heidi, like us, got discouraged when the answer did not come right away.

"Do you pray to Him every day," Grandmamma asked, "to make you happy again?"

"No, not any more."

"I'm sorry to hear that. Why have you stopped?"

"It's no use. God didn't hear me and I daresay that if all the people in Frankfurt pray for things at the same time, He can't notice everybody and I'm sure He didn't hear me."

"Why are you so sure?"

"I prayed the same prayer every day for a long time and nothing happened."

"It isn't quite like that, Heidi," Grandmamma explained, and she went on to tell Heidi that sometimes God *waits* before answering our prayers. "He has been watching over you," Grandmamma told her, "all this time—never doubt that—but you have stopped praying, and that showed you did not really believe in Him."[19]

We can't quit asking. We ask, and ask again. We seek, and seek again. We knock, and knock again. This is what Dorothy did, abandoned in Oz. She asked, "What am I going to do?"

And by asking, we're brought right back to where we started, an Orphan again. The inner journey isn't linear, learning our lessons and chalking them off, it's cyclical, like monopoly. We go round and round, making and remaking choices, and each time around—Orphan, Pilgrim, Martyr, Warrior, Wizard—we learn just a little bit more of who we are.

So this is all there is? Just endless trials and tribulations, landing on Boardwalk, never finding redemption, Eden or Kansas or happily ever after? Abandoned like Dorothy with Toto in Oz? Asking one more time, "Oh, Scarecrow, what am I going to do?"

Punch the rewind. "Oh, Scarecrow, what am I going to do?"

"Look!" he says.

We gasp. The pretty pink bubble! And down floats the good witch Glinda.

No. This is not all there is.

NOTES

1. Robert Munsch, *The Paper Bag Princess* (Toronto: Annick Press, 1981).

2. Not her real name.

3. John 8:32 (paraphrased) (NIV).

4. Matthew 10:16 (NIV).

5. Zora Neale Hurston, *MOSES Man Of The Mountain* (New York: J.B. Lippincott, 1939), 11.

6. Hurston, *MOSES Man Of The Mountain,* 39.

7. Genesis 38:18 (KJV, paraphrased).

8. Elizabeth Gaskell, *Cranford* (England: Chapman and Hall and Smith Elder, 1853).

9. E.M. Montgomery, *Anne of Green Gables* (L.C. Page & Company. Renewal copyright © 1935 by L.C. Page & Co. Reprinted by permission of Farrar, Straus and Giroux, Inc.) Bantam edition, 64, 65.

10. Montgomery, *Anne of Green Gables,* Bantam edition, 75, 76.

11. Laura Ingalls Wilder, *Little Town on the Prairie* (New York: Harper & Row, 1971), 99–105.

12. I Samuel 25:24 (NIV).

13. Cornelius Plantiga, Jr., "Maze of Hearts," *Christianity Today,* 19 March 1990, 19.

14. Carol Pearson, *The Hero Within* (San Francisco: Harper & Row, 1986), 125.

15. 1 John 1:8, 9 (RSV).

16. 2 Corinthians 5:17 (KJV).

17. Not her real name.

18. John Fischer, *True Believers Don't Ask Why* (Minneapolis: Bethany House, 1989), 12.

19. Johanna Spyri, *Heidi* (England: Penguin Books, 1956), 108, 109.

EIGHT ... *L*IVING HAPPILY EVER AFTER

Last night I got a phone call from my friend who, coincidentally enough, lives in Kansas. Why is life always so hard? she asked. Why all this trouble, why all this pain, why all this grief? Why, my friend was asking, all the dragons? Where is the hero and redemption we seek? Why are we left behind when all we really want is to get back to Kansas, back to Uncle Henry and Auntie Em? *Where is the happily ever after of our fairy tales?*

Let's go back to Dorothy in *The Wizard of Oz*. She's stranded, remember? The Wizard has taken off for Kansas without her and she's in absolute despair. We can certainly relate. Will we never get home? Will we never get back to Kansas? Will we never live happily ever after?

But wait. Do our fairy tales really promise happily ever after without disappointment? Without dragons? This is the assumption we're making, isn't it? That to live happily ever after is to live without pain and conflict?

But tell me, did Cinderella live happily ever after without a struggle? Did Sleeping Beauty live happily ever after without trauma? Did Rapunzel live happily ever after without grief? Did Hansel and Gretel live happily ever after without deprivation? Did Jack and the beanstalk live happily ever after without risk? Did Thumbelina live happily ever after without sacrifice? Are there any fairy tales without *any* dragons?

Where in the world, then, did we ever get the notion that to live happily ever after means to live without trouble? For when we look at fairy tales we find it's not the absence of dragons—but the *taming* of dragons—that ushers in happily ever after.

Do you know anyone who seems to have lived pretty much without dragons, everything handed to them—health, good looks, intelligence, money, golden opportunities all delivered on a silver platter? Compare them to those who've really come up against hard times. Compare Scrooge to Tiny Tim.

Recently I've become involved with wheelchair athletes. Ken, with a head injury, has to lie flat on his back, helpless, while we take off his leg brace and tug on a dry suit. But it's a Fonzie's thumbs up and a wild grin when we get him onto the water and into the sit-ski. Doug Taylor is a walking quad and because he has so little grip in his hands I have to practically sit in his lap to pull his dry suit on over his feet. We laugh, we look so silly. But Doug is the 1991 national champion for quadriplegics in water ski competition and the only quad in the world who can jump the KAN-SKI.

There is no doubt about it, Tiny Tim understands something old Scrooge took a long time figuring out. It's not the absence of dragons that brings about happiness; it's the taming of them. And if we're going to be honest about it, instead of fanciful, we know this to be absolutely true.

But back to Dorothy. "Oh, will you help me?" she pleads when Glinda, the good Witch of the North, appears in the pretty pink bubble only moments after the Wizard vanishes. "Can you help me?" But what does Glinda say? Turn the video on and let's listen.

"You don't need to be helped any longer. You've always had the power to go back to Kansas."

"I have?" Dorothy says. *We have?* we ask.

And here is another misconception we all seem to have when it comes to living happily ever after. Happiness is not dependent upon some knight in shining armor we're still looking for or a charming prince riding in to rescue. *We are our own heroes.* It's *we* who have the power to get back to Kansas, to live happily ever after. It's our choice. It's us, you and me.

We may balk at the news. We'd really rather keep searching for a more glorious hero, as did Naman with his leprosy and the Jews with the Messiah. But go back to the fairy tales and see how mistaken we've been. Where would Cinderella be if she'd not first been her own hero and stood up to her wicked stepmother? Where would Jack be if he'd just gawked at the beanstalk instead of first being his own hero and climbing the thing? And Gretel? Where would she be if she'd not first been her own hero and given Hansel a bone with which to trick the witch?

How did we get this all so mixed up? Where would *any* of our fairy-tale folk be if they'd not first been their own heroes? Victims, like many of us—cleaning out cinders, going hungry, and getting baked into gingerbread. *It isn't until we choose to become our own heroes that the princes and knights and fairy godmothers can make their move.* Glinda in *The Wizard of Oz* is right. It *is* we who hold the power to go back to Kansas. *We* choose our happily ever after.

"Then why didn't you tell her before?" the Scarecrow demands—*and so do we.* Why the promise of a Wizard if we're to save ourselves? Why the yellow brick road if we could have avoided it? Why the wicked witch to make things so difficult? *Why all the dragons?*

Glinda has an answer. Dorothy had to take her journey along the yellow brick road because, unless put to the test, she would not have believed she *could* be her own hero, that happiness *was* her choice. "She wouldn't have believed me," Glinda tells the Scarecrow. "She had to learn it for herself."

Wait, wait a minute. Punch the rewind.

She wouldn't have believed me. She had to learn it for herself.

*Reeee*wind! One more time.

She wouldn't have believed me. She had to learn it for herself.

Tell me, are we any different?

Last year I had a big party and invited all my friends. I was celebrating everything I'd accomplished in the eight years since my divorce: my B.A., my M.A., my teaching, the completion of a fifth book, a contract for three more. Eight years ago I'd had none of these things. In fact, eight years ago I'd been a total basket case. My sister, remember, used to ask, "Brenda, what can I do to help?" and I used to whimper, "I don't know, just please help me." Two years of college, limited job experience, one unpublished novel, poor health, three little kids. I'd been over the edge and dangling. Yet today I've accomplished all that I'd set out to do, and more. How, I asked myself while visiting with family and friends who'd come to help celebrate, did it happen? How?

In looking back (down the yellow brick road) the answer is astonishingly clear. The dragons. The moment I'd decided to quit enduring the monsters and confront them instead, I, like Dorothy, had been snatched from Kansas and tossed into Oz, where I'd been forced (kicking and screaming and spiraling out of control half the time) to tame those dragons—first as Orphan, then Pilgrim, then Martyr, Warrior, and Wizard, until I evolved into a woman that I, eight years ago, would never have believed possible, not even if God himself had come down for tea to forewarn me. Like Dorothy, I had to learn it for myself, and it took the dragons and the yellow brick road to teach me.

It puts a new perspective on our troubles, doesn't it? Dragons aren't the enemy we envisioned. They propel us forward (albeit kicking and screaming and sometimes spiraling out of control) into the redemption we seek. We have every reason to be thankful, and if we wonder why all the dragons, why all the heartache and grief, why the yellow brick road, it's because we, like Dorothy, have yet to learn that even though the dragons reign it's our choice to go back to Kansas, to live happily ever after. It's always our choice.

"What have you learned?" the Scarecrow asks Dorothy.

"That it wasn't enough to just want to see Uncle Henry and Auntie Em," she tells them all. "And it's that if I ever go looking for my heart's desire I won't look any further than my own backyard. Because if it isn't there, I never really lost it to begin with."

Do you see what Dorothy has learned? She is her own hero. She's learned that her heart's desire, her happily ever after, is not something she can find by looking or that anyone can give to her. It's not somewhere over the rainbow, "where troubles melt like lemon drops," but rather, her happily ever after is something she must choose for herself. More than that, *her happily ever after lies in the midst of trouble, in her own backyard where Miss Gulch awaits, basket over arm, sheriff's warrant in hand, for Toto.*

Miss Gulch . . . We forgot about Miss Gulch. We got so busy thinking that if we could just get back home, if we could just find Uncle Henry and Auntie Em, everything would be all right. But it won't. It isn't.

But does it matter, though?

Ma Ingalls told Laura when she found Spanish needle grass on the prairie that this earthly life is a battle. "It always has been so," she said, sewing pins between her lips, "and it always will be. The sooner you make up your mind the better off you'll be, and the more thankful for your pleasures. Now Mary, I'm ready to fit the bodice."[1]

Scott Peck echoes her sentiments when he states his premise at the very beginning of his book. "Once we truly know that life is difficult," he writes, "once we truly understand and accept it—then life is no longer difficult. Because once it is accepted, the fact that life is difficult no longer matters."[2]

It no longer matters because Miss Gulch is inconsequential. Redemption, remember, lies not in the ab-

sence of dragons, but in the taming of them—and
Dorothy knows now she can do it. She is, after all,
Orphan, Pilgrim, Martyr, Warrior, and Wizard. She is,
she has learned, her own hero.

Words, though. When the dragon strikes, we crum-
ble, and it all becomes just words. In January 1976 my
doctor told me I would lose the baby I was carrying,
and while I could understand in my mind that it's my
choice to find happiness amidst my pain, I couldn't
make it work. The dragon roared and all logic and
intellect, theory, philosophy, and theology went right
out the window. A friend came over. She had miscar-
ried the year before and she tried to remind me of
everything we gain from disappointment.

"I have a better understanding of God's love," she
told me. "So much so that I'm truly grateful for the
experience."

I listened, but it was all empty words, words that
meant nothing to me. I only wanted my baby.

But then Ellen opened the Bible and gave me a
verse, a promise from God.

"And now those magic slippers," says Glinda, "will
take you back home in two seconds."

The magic slippers. The ruby shoes, symbols of liberty and safety in the midst of chaos, our promise that
God is with us. It makes all the difference in the
world, for it's the ruby shoes that transport us where
we need to be.

Dorothy looks down. The ruby shoes sparkle and
glisten.

I looked down and read for myself God's promise.

Blessed be God, even the Father of our Lord Jesus Christ,
the Father of mercies, and the God of all comfort; Who
comforteth us in all our tribulation, that we may be able
to comfort them which are in any trouble, by the comfort wherewith we ourselves are comforted of God.[3]

"Tap your heels three times," says Glinda.

"Are you sure God will comfort me?" I asked Ellen.

"Yes," she said, and when I looked into her eyes I knew she spoke the truth. He had done it for her. He would do it for me. Miss Gulch? It didn't matter that she waited. That she was going to take away Toto. I was wearing the ruby shoes, and God would go with me.

"And say, there's no place like home."

"There's no place like home. There's no place . . ."

Is this the music we'd first heard when Miss Gulch came riding her bike down the dusty road? It doesn't matter.

"There's no place like home. . . . There's no place like home. . . ."

I lost my baby, but the peace that passeth all understanding caught me where I was and took me home, right to the very heart of God.

Yes, once upon a time the dragon roared and continues to roar, but when we're wearing God's ruby shoes we can, and do, overcome.

The choice is ours.

This is living happily ever after.

NOTES

1. Laura Ingalls Wilder, *Little Town on the Prairie* (New York: Harper & Row, 1971), 89, 90.

2. M. Scott Peck, *The Road Less Traveled* (New York: Simon & Schuster, 1978), 15.

3. 2 Corinthians 1:3, 4 (KJV).

ℬIBLIOGRAPHY

Alsdurf, James and Phyllis. *Battered Into Submission,* quoted in "Battered Into Submission," *Christianity Today,* 16 June 1989.

Banner, Lois. "Elizabeth Cady Stanton: Early Marriage and Feminist Rebellion," in Linda K. Kerber and Jane DeHart-Mathews, eds., *Woman's America* (New York: Oxford University Press, 1987).

Baum, Frank. *The Wizard of Oz* film, Turner Entertainment Co. 1939 by Lowe's Co. 1966 Metro-Goldwyn-Mayer Inc.

Belle, Deborah. *Lives in Stress* (Los Angeles: Sage, 1982).

Bible, the.

Blockson, Charles L. *The Underground Railroad* (New York: Berkeley, 1989).

Bronte, Charlotte. *Jane Eyre* (New York: New American Library, 1987).

Bunyon, John. *The Pilgrim's Progress* (Old Tappan, NJ: Revel, 1977).

Cirlot, J. E. *A Dictionary of Symbols* (New York: Philosophical Library, 1962).

Coleman, Judge H. Joseph, Chair. *Findings of the Washington State Task Force on Gender and Justice in the Courts* (Olympia, WA, 1989).

Deen, Elizabeth. *All The Women of the Bible* (San Francisco: Harper-Collins, 1955).

Disney, Walt. *Cinderella* video.

Disney, Walt. *Dumbo* video.

Dobson, James C. *Love Must Be Tough* (Waco, TX: Word, 1983).

Euripides. *Medea.*

Fischer, John. *True Believers Don't Ask Why* (Minneapolis: Bethany House, 1989).

Gaskell, Elizabeth. *Cranford* (England: Chapman and Hall and Smith Elder, 1853).

Hansel, Tim. *You Gotta Keep Dancin'* (Elgin, IL: David C. Cook, 1985).

Houston, James M. "The Independence Myth," *Christianity Today,* 15 January 1990.

Hurston, Zora Neale. *Their Eyes Were Watching God* (New York: HarperCollins, 1937).

Hurston, Zora Neale. *MOSES Man Of The Mountain* (New York: HarperCollins, 1939).

Johnston, Johanna. *Runaway to Heaven* (Garden City, NY: Doubleday, 1963).

Jones, Rufus. *The Quakers in the American Colonies* (New York: W. W. Norton Co. Inc., 1986).

Josephus, Flavius. *Life and Works.*

Koehler, Lyle. "The Case of the American Jezebels," in Linda K. Kerber and Jane DeHart-Mathews, eds., *Woman's America* (New York: Oxford University Press, 1987).

Larson, Bruce. *Ask Me To Dance* (Waco, TX: Word, 1972), 16.

Larson, Bruce. *There's A Lot More To Health Than Not Being Sick* (Waco, TX: Word, 1981).

L'Engle, Madeleine. *A Wrinkle In Time* (New York: Farrar, Straus & Giroux, Inc., 1982).

Lerner, Harriet Goldhor. *The Dance of Anger* (New York: HarperCollins, 1986).

Link, Terry. "Original Red Riding Hood now a wimp, scholar reports," *The Tribune,* 8 September 1989.

Marshall, Catherine. *Christy* (New York: McGraw-Hill, 1967).

Massachusetts Colony, Record Of

Montgomery, E. M. *Anne of Green Gables* (New York: Farrar, Straus and Giroux, Inc., 1935).

Munsch, Robert. *A Paper Bag Princess* (Toronto: Annick Press, 1981).

Nixon, Eva S. "Mary Counts Miracles in Her Night of Terror," *UPC Times,* vol. 9, no. 4 (July 1989).

Olson, Esther Lee and Peterson, Ken. *No Place To Hide* (Wheaton: Tyndale, 1980).

O'Neil, Dennis. *Secret Origins of the Super Heroes* (n.p., n.d.).

Ortiz, Virginia. *Sojourner Truth: A Self Made Woman* (New York: HarperCollins, 1974).

Palmer, Marion. *Walt Disney's Uncle Remus Stories* (New York: Golden Press, 1946).

Pearson, Carol. *The Hero Within* (San Francisco: Harper & Row, 1986).

Peck, M. Scott. *The Road Less Traveled* (New York: Simon & Schuster, 1978).

Peck, M. Scott. *People of the Lie* (New York: Simon & Schuster, 1983).

Plantiga, Cornelius, Jr. "Maze of Hearts," *Christianity Today,* 19 March 1990.

Prince, Mary. "The History of Mary Prince" in Henry Louis Gates, Jr., ed., *The Classic Slave Narrations* (New York: New American Library, 1987).

Reifert, Gail and Dermody, Eugene. *Women Who Fought: An American History* (Reifert and Dermody, 1978).

Seattle Times, 8 November 1988.

Sherrill, John and Elizabeth. *The Hiding Place* (Old Tappan, NJ: Chosen Books, 1987).

Sidel, Ruth. *Women and Children Last* (New York: Viking Penguin, 1986).

Spyri, Johanna. *Heidi* (England: Penguin, 1956).

Stanton, Elizabeth Cady. "Declaration of Sentiments" in Susan B. Anthony and Melissa Joslyn Gage, eds., *History of Woman Suffrage* (New York: Flower & Wells, 1881).

Stowe, Harriet Beecher. *Uncle Tom's Cabin, or Life Among The Lowly* (Boston: John P. Jewett, 1852).

U.S. Bureau of the Census Report, P-60, no. 146.

Walker, Lenore E. *The Battered Woman* (New York: Harper & Row, 1979).

Weitzman, Lenore. *The Divorce Revolution* (New York: The Free Press, 1987).

White, E. B. *Charlotte's Web* (New York: HarperCollins, 1952).

Wilbee, Brenda. "Part of The Family," *Moody Monthly,* October 1987.

Wilder, Laura Ingalls. *On the Banks of Plum Creek* (New York: HarperCollins, 1971).

Wilder, Laura Ingalls. *Little Town on the Prairie* (New York: Harper-Collins, 1971).